The CBT
Art Workbook
for Managing Stress

Part of the CBT Art Workbooks for Mental and Emotional Wellbeing series

The CBT Art Workbooks for Mental and Emotional Wellbeing series provides creative CBT information and worksheets for adults to manage and understand a variety of emotional issues. Suitable for adults in individual or group therapeutic work, they are an excellent resource to use in conjunction with professional therapy or for adults to use themselves to improve and maintain mental wellbeing.

Also part of the CBT Art Workbooks for Mental and Emotional Wellbeing series

The CBT Art Workbook for Coping with Anxiety
Jennifer Guest
ISBN 978 1 78775 012 8
eISBN 978 1 78775 013 5

The CBT Art Workbook for Coping with Depression
Jennifer Guest
ISBN 978 1 78775 096 8
eISBN 978 1 78775 097 5

The CBT Art Workbook for Managing Anger
Jennifer Guest
ISBN 978 1 78775 100 2
eISBN 978 1 78775 101 9

By the same author

The Art Activity Book for Psychotherapeutic Work
100 Illustrated CBT and Psychodynamic Handouts for Creative Therapeutic Work
Jennifer Guest
ISBN 978 1 78592 301 2
eISBN 978 1 78450 607 0

The Art Activity Book for Relational Work
100 illustrated therapeutic worksheets to use with individuals, couples and families
Jennifer Guest
ISBN 978 1 78592 160 5
eISBN 978 1 78450 428 1

The CBT Art Activity Book
100 illustrated handouts for creative therapeutic work
Jennifer Guest
ISBN 978 1 84905 665 6
eISBN 978 1 78450 168 6

The CBT
Art Workbook
for Managing Stress

Part of the CBT Art Workbooks for Mental
and Emotional Wellbeing *series*

Jennifer Guest

Jessica Kingsley Publishers
London and Philadelphia

First published in 2020
by Jessica Kingsley Publishers
73 Collier Street
London N1 9BE, UK
and
400 Market Street, Suite 400
Philadelphia, PA 19106, USA

www.jkp.com

Library of Congress Cataloging in Publication Data
A CIP catalog record for this book is available from the Library of Congress

British Library Cataloguing in Publication Data
A CIP catalogue record for this book is available from the British Library

ISBN 978 1 78775 098 2
eISBN 978 1 78775 099 9

Printed and bound in the United States

Acknowledgements

I would like to express many thanks to all my clients and colleagues, who, over the years have helped bring this workbook into being. Grateful appreciation goes to the theorists who have devoted their lives and careers to helping people experience happier, healthier and more peaceful lives. I've given credit to theorists where I've knowingly designed a worksheet from their work, and there are some pages designed from techniques I've come across over the years which I'm unfortunately unable to give specific credit to. No worksheets have been created where the source of the credit is known and not mentioned. Thanks also to everyone involved at Jessica Kingsley Publishers for their support and input.

Contents

About This Book

This workbook offers an opportunity for those experiencing high stress levels to help manage and cope with the symptoms, using tools from cognitive behavioural therapy (CBT) approaches.

I've worked with many clients experiencing stress over the years, and have found CBT ideas have been incredibly successful in helping to reduce symptoms, as well as for learning ways to help manage them. It's a privilege to be able to share these ideas with you here, and I sincerely hope this workbook has a positive impact on your life and your wellbeing.

This book can be used autonomously or in conjunction with therapy. It's not intended to be used as a replacement for cognitive behavioural therapy if therapeutic input would be beneficial. Please ensure that access to professional support is available if you experience any unexpected or overwhelming emotional reactions as a result of working through this book, or your symptoms become more severe.

You might choose to focus on the pages most relevant to you, or work through the entire book from beginning to end.

Introduction

INTRODUCTION

This workbook follows steps used in CBT.

These aim to:

- Explore the nature of the problem
- Gather information by monitoring levels of stress experienced
- Recognise the links between thoughts, emotions, physiological responses and behaviour
- Explore unhelpful thinking patterns, beliefs and behaviours
- Teach how to implement positive and realistic thinking and reactions

These steps help us to develop healthy behaviours and thought patterns, to increase our emotional wellbeing, in order to more effectively manage times of stress.

WHY ART?

Having worked within the therapeutic world for nearly two decades, I consider delivering therapy as one of my passions, alongside art.

Making art has been personally therapeutic during times when I've experienced emotional challenges and high levels of stress in my life.

I've witnessed the benefits of art-making and using visual ways of expression and processing with many clients. At the very least, this is a way to encourage relaxation, and, on a more profound level, it can facilitate deeper change. The ideas in this workbook provide a focus for coping with and reducing harmful stress levels through the use of creativity.

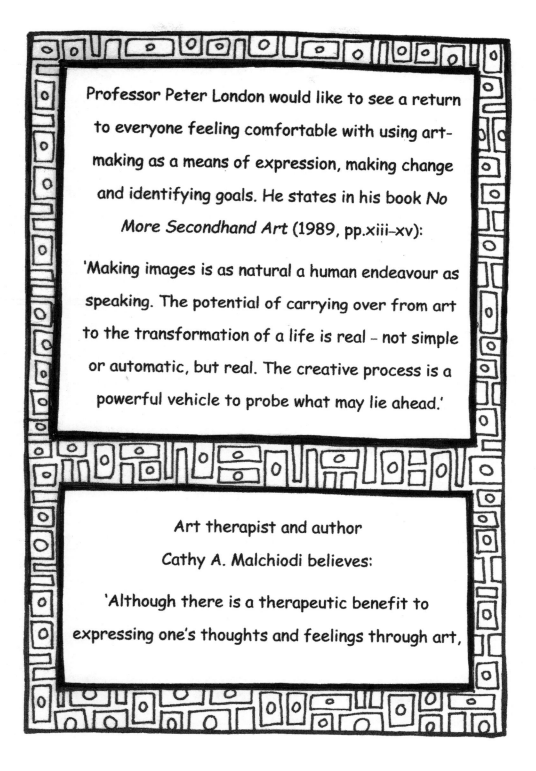

Professor Peter London would like to see a return to everyone feeling comfortable with using art-making as a means of expression, making change and identifying goals. He states in his book *No More Secondhand Art* (1989, pp.xiii–xv):

'Making images is as natural a human endeavour as speaking. The potential of carrying over from art to the transformation of a life is real – not simple or automatic, but real. The creative process is a powerful vehicle to probe what may lie ahead.'

Art therapist and author
Cathy A. Malchiodi believes:

'Although there is a therapeutic benefit to expressing one's thoughts and feelings through art,

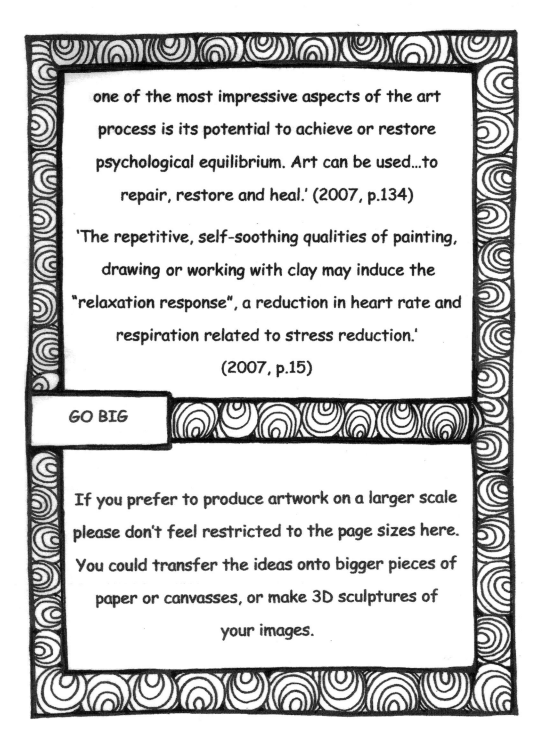

one of the most impressive aspects of the art process is its potential to achieve or restore psychological equilibrium. Art can be used...to repair, restore and heal.' (2007, p.134)

'The repetitive, self-soothing qualities of painting, drawing or working with clay may induce the "relaxation response", a reduction in heart rate and respiration related to stress reduction.'

(2007, p.15)

GO BIG

If you prefer to produce artwork on a larger scale please don't feel restricted to the page sizes here. You could transfer the ideas onto bigger pieces of paper or canvasses, or make 3D sculptures of your images.

1

What Is Stress?

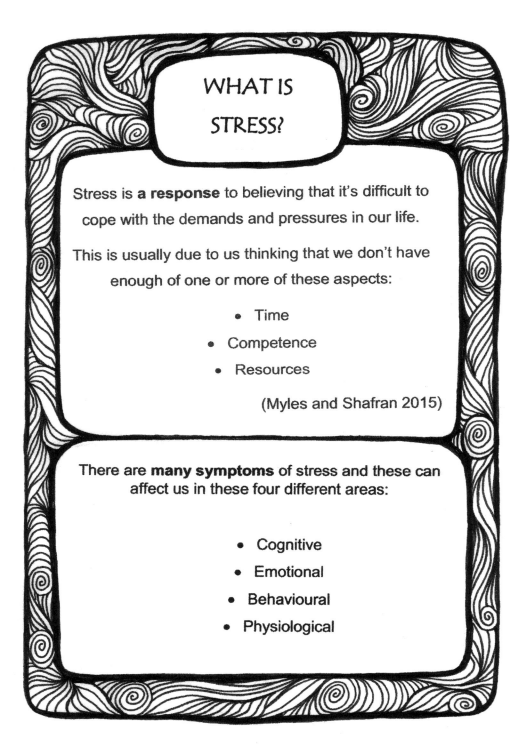

WHAT IS STRESS?

Stress is **a response** to believing that it's difficult to cope with the demands and pressures in our life.

This is usually due to us thinking that we don't have enough of one or more of these aspects:

- Time
- Competence
- Resources

(Myles and Shafran 2015)

There are **many symptoms** of stress and these can affect us in these four different areas:

- Cognitive
- Emotional
- Behavioural
- Physiological

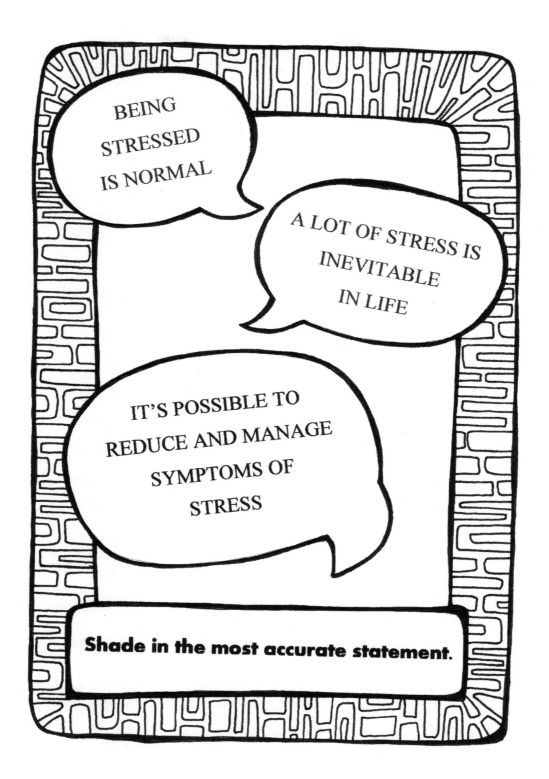

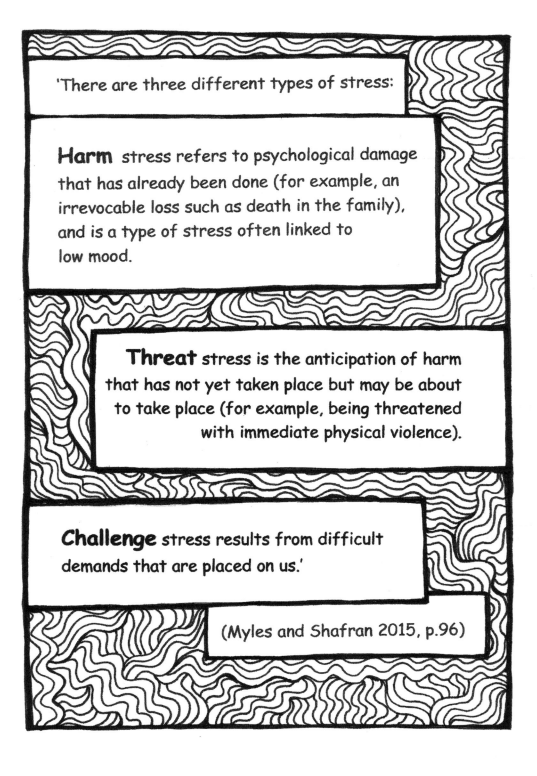

'There are three different types of stress:

Harm stress refers to psychological damage that has already been done (for example, an irrevocable loss such as death in the family), and is a type of stress often linked to low mood.

Threat stress is the anticipation of harm that has not yet taken place but may be about to take place (for example, being threatened with immediate physical violence).

Challenge stress results from difficult demands that are placed on us.'

(Myles and Shafran 2015, p.96)

WHAT CAUSES STRESS?

External factors

- Tense or distressing situations or interactions

- Changing circumstances

- Criticism

- Conflict

- Pressure

- Threats of physical or emotional harm

Internal factors

- Health issues

- Medical procedures

- Emotional problems

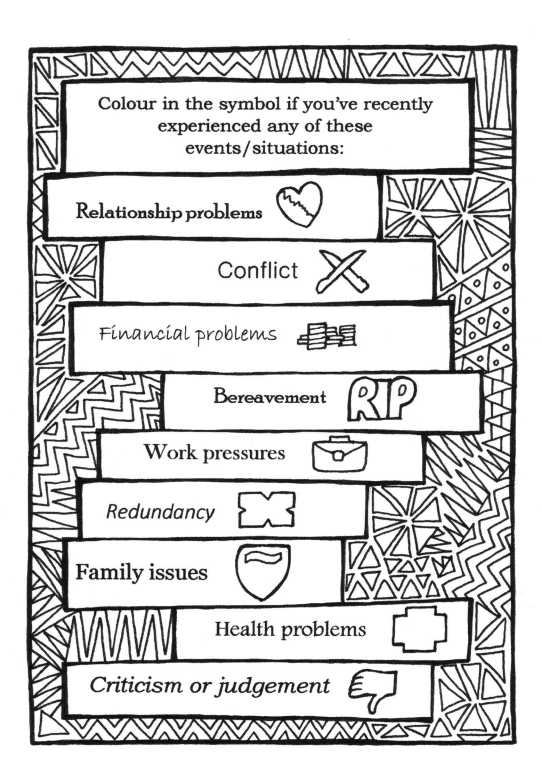

Colour in the symbol if you've recently experienced any of these events/situations:

Relationship problems

Conflict

Financial problems

Bereavement RIP

Work pressures

Redundancy

Family issues

Health problems

Criticism or judgement

Going on holiday

Organising a celebration

Becoming a parent

Events that we welcome and are positive can also make us feel stressed!

Shade over any of these you've experienced and found stressful:

Starting a new job

Getting married

Family gatherings

Moving house

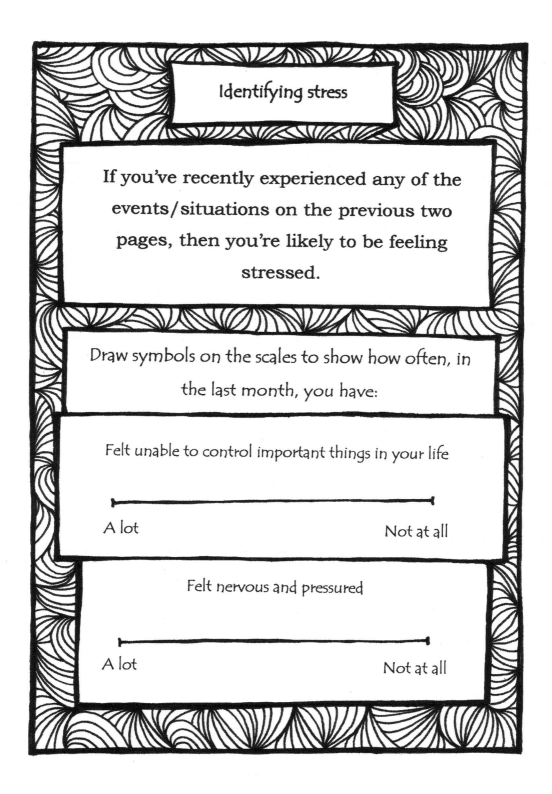

Identifying stress

If you've recently experienced any of the events/situations on the previous two pages, then you're likely to be feeling stressed.

Draw symbols on the scales to show how often, in the last month, you have:

Felt unable to control important things in your life

A lot   Not at all

Felt nervous and pressured

A lot   Not at all

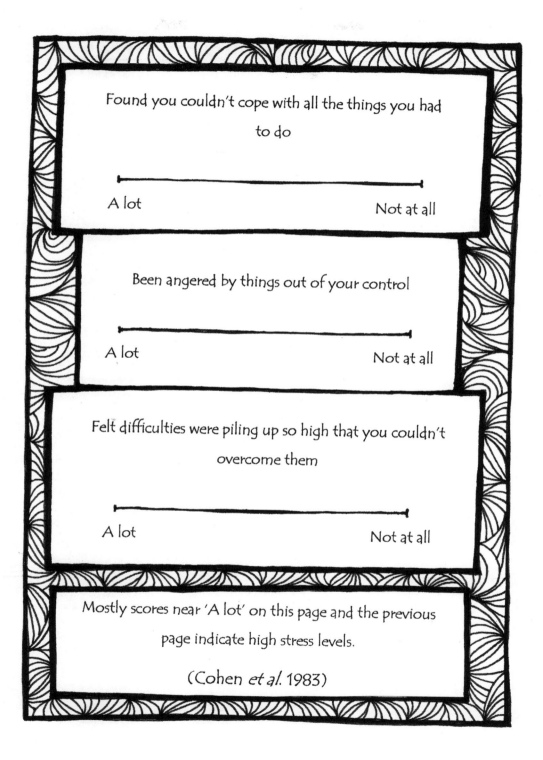

Found you couldn't cope with all the things you had to do

A lot   Not at all

Been angered by things out of your control

A lot   Not at all

Felt difficulties were piling up so high that you couldn't overcome them

A lot   Not at all

Mostly scores near 'A lot' on this page and the previous page indicate high stress levels.

(Cohen *et al.* 1983)

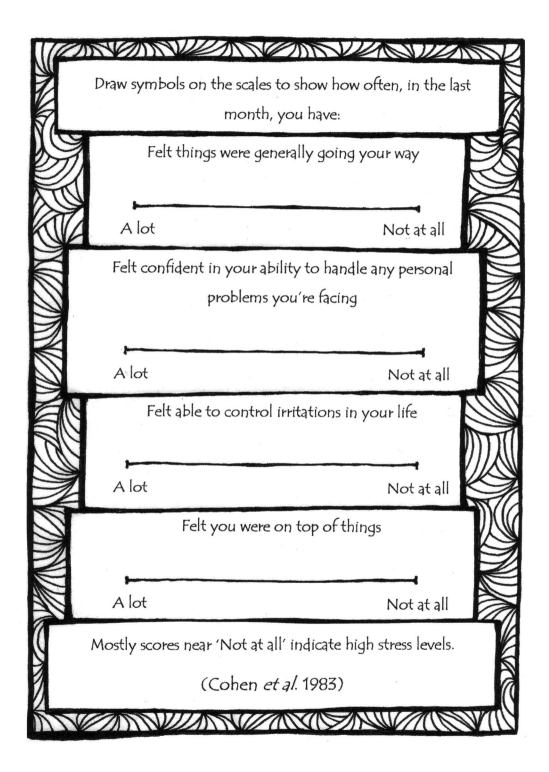

Draw symbols on the scales to show how often, in the last month, you have:

Felt things were generally going your way

A lot   Not at all

Felt confident in your ability to handle any personal problems you're facing

A lot   Not at all

Felt able to control irritations in your life

A lot   Not at all

Felt you were on top of things

A lot   Not at all

Mostly scores near 'Not at all' indicate high stress levels.

(Cohen *et al.* 1983)

A small amount of stress can be healthy, especially if we need to meet a deadline, complete a task, or respond immediately to a threat. Prolonged stress can be damaging for our physical and mental health, and it can be easy to become accustomed to being stressed so that it starts to feel normal.

It can often reach a crisis point before we're able to gain awareness of the impact on our health and wellbeing.

What one person finds stressful can be completely different for someone else, who may find the same situation/experience stimulating or enjoyable. We might also find something stressful at a certain point in our life, and not feel stressed about it at another time.

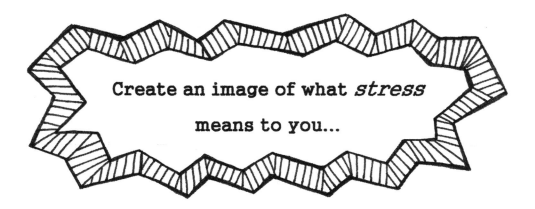

Create an image of what *stress* means to you...

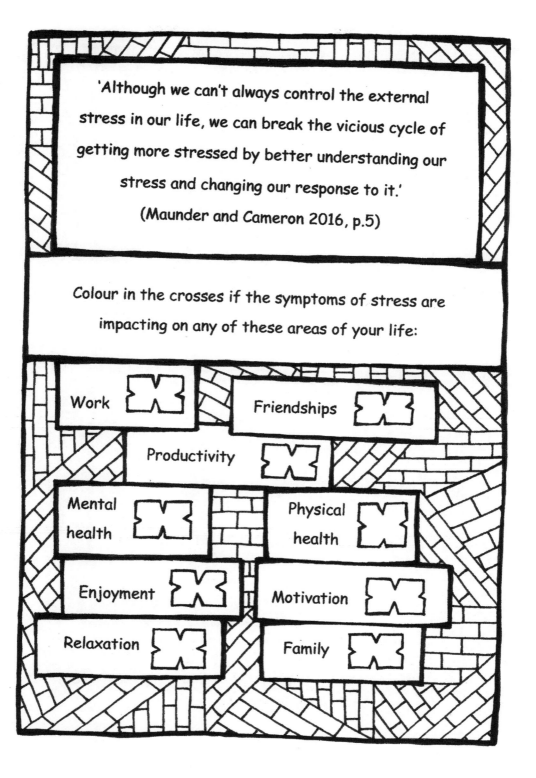

'Although we can't always control the external stress in our life, we can break the vicious cycle of getting more stressed by better understanding our stress and changing our response to it.'
(Maunder and Cameron 2016, p.5)

Colour in the crosses if the symptoms of stress are impacting on any of these areas of your life:

Work

Friendships

Productivity

Mental health

Physical health

Enjoyment

Motivation

Relaxation

Family

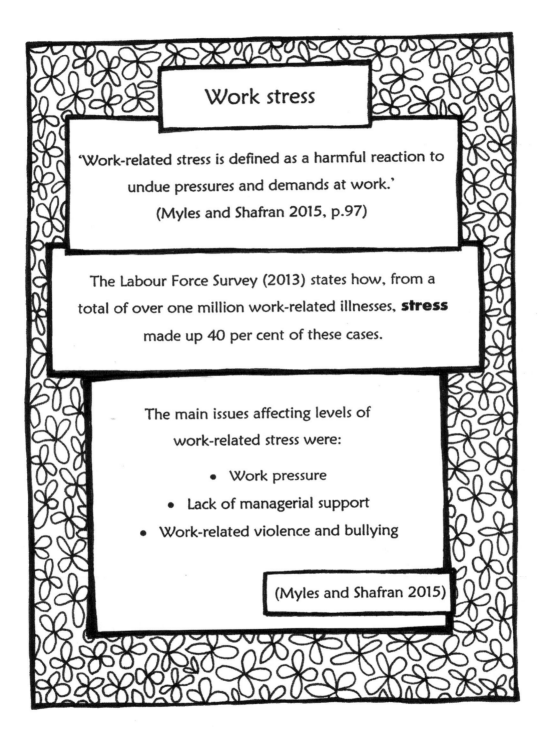

Work stress

'Work-related stress is defined as a harmful reaction to undue pressures and demands at work.'
(Myles and Shafran 2015, p.97)

The Labour Force Survey (2013) states how, from a total of over one million work-related illnesses, **stress** made up 40 per cent of these cases.

The main issues affecting levels of work-related stress were:

- Work pressure
- Lack of managerial support
- Work-related violence and bullying

(Myles and Shafran 2015)

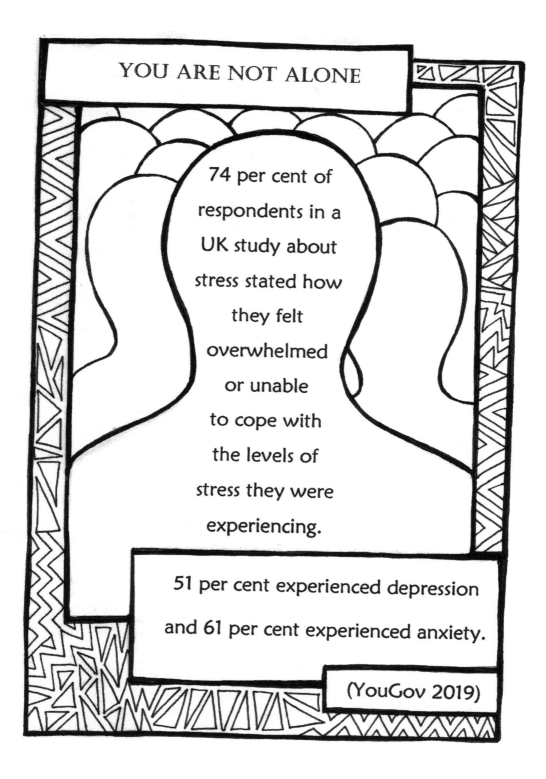

YOU ARE NOT ALONE

74 per cent of respondents in a UK study about stress stated how they felt overwhelmed or unable to cope with the levels of stress they were experiencing.

51 per cent experienced depression and 61 per cent experienced anxiety.

(YouGov 2019)

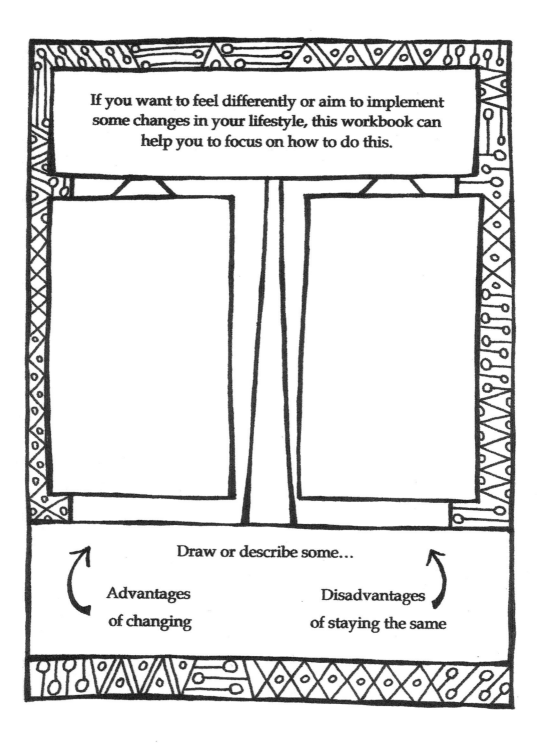

If you want to feel differently or aim to implement some changes in your lifestyle, this workbook can help you to focus on how to do this.

Draw or describe some...

Advantages
of changing

Disadvantages
of staying the same

2

What Is CBT?

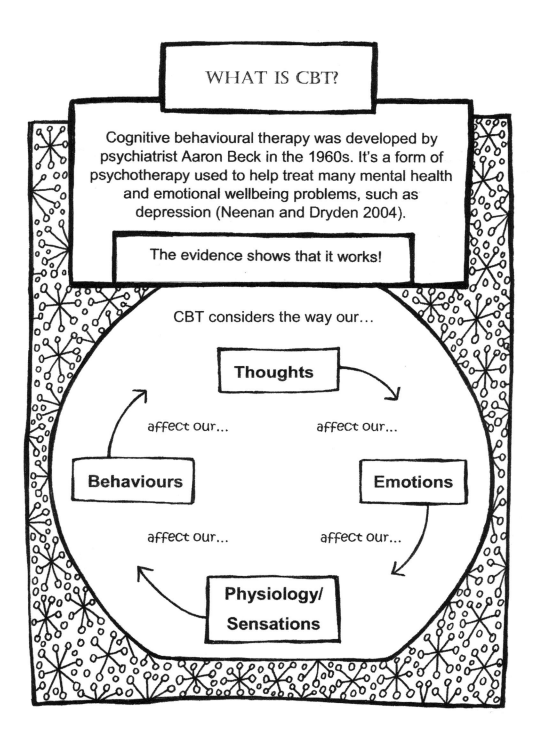

WHAT IS CBT?

Cognitive behavioural therapy was developed by psychiatrist Aaron Beck in the 1960s. It's a form of psychotherapy used to help treat many mental health and emotional wellbeing problems, such as depression (Neenan and Dryden 2004).

The evidence shows that it works!

CBT considers the way our...

Thoughts

affect our...

affect our...

Behaviours

Emotions

affect our...

affect our...

Physiology/ Sensations

'The aim of CBT techniques is to disrupt negative thought patterns, so they no longer arouse unbearable emotions.

Recognising thoughts as "just thoughts", rather them mistaking them for true perceptions or impulses that must be acted on, produces a calmer, more positive state of mind.'

(Barford 2018, p.35)

Stress can be intensified by thinking negatively about our:

✓ Selves

✓ Achievements

✓ Ability to cope

✓ Capacity to access help/support

✓ Future accomplishments

✓ Health

Colour in the ticks if any of these are the focus of negative thinking for you.

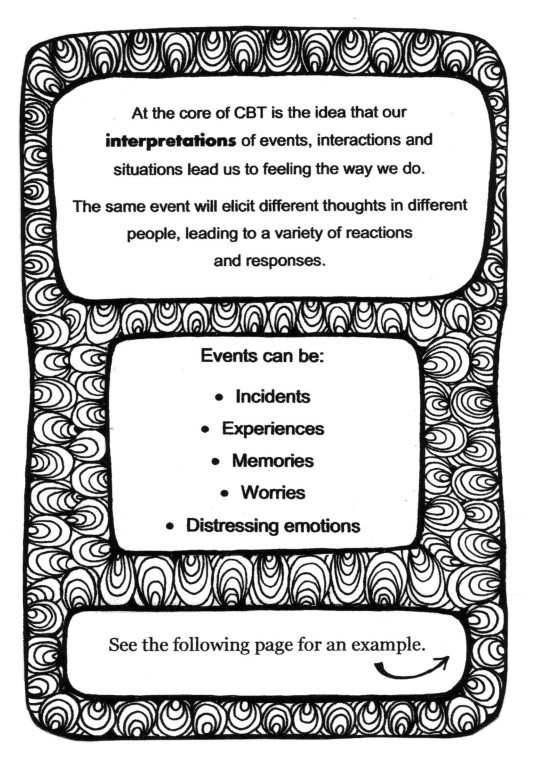

At the core of CBT is the idea that our **interpretations** of events, interactions and situations lead us to feeling the way we do.

The same event will elicit different thoughts in different people, leading to a variety of reactions and responses.

Events can be:

- Incidents
- Experiences
- Memories
- Worries
- Distressing emotions

See the following page for an example.

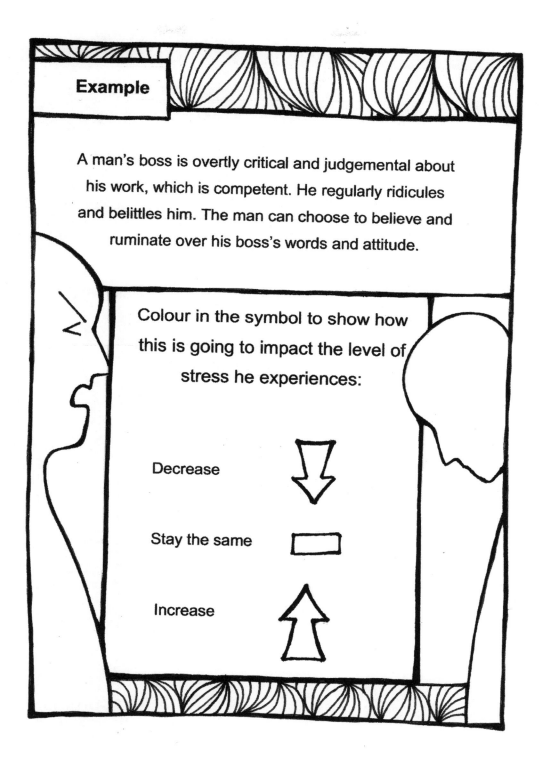

Example

A man's boss is overtly critical and judgemental about his work, which is competent. He regularly ridicules and belittles him. The man can choose to believe and ruminate over his boss's words and attitude.

Colour in the symbol to show how this is going to impact the level of stress he experiences:

Decrease

Stay the same

Increase

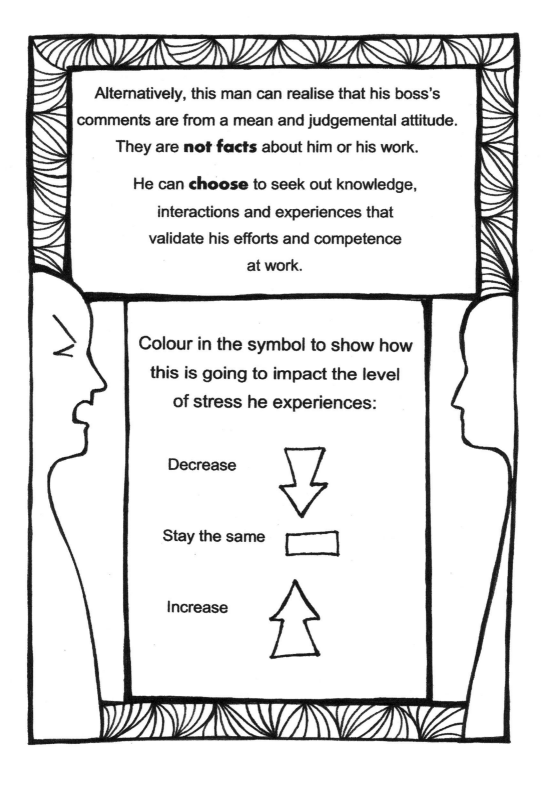

Alternatively, this man can realise that his boss's comments are from a mean and judgemental attitude. They are **not facts** about him or his work.

He can **choose** to seek out knowledge, interactions and experiences that validate his efforts and competence at work.

Colour in the symbol to show how this is going to impact the level of stress he experiences:

Decrease

Stay the same

Increase

3

Observations

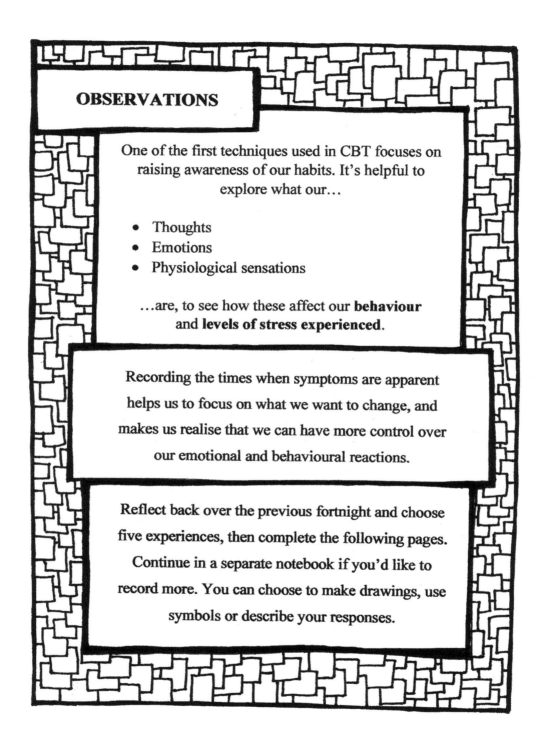

OBSERVATIONS

One of the first techniques used in CBT focuses on raising awareness of our habits. It's helpful to explore what our...

- Thoughts
- Emotions
- Physiological sensations

...are, to see how these affect our **behaviour** and **levels of stress experienced**.

Recording the times when symptoms are apparent helps us to focus on what we want to change, and makes us realise that we can have more control over our emotional and behavioural reactions.

Reflect back over the previous fortnight and choose five experiences, then complete the following pages. Continue in a separate notebook if you'd like to record more. You can choose to make drawings, use symbols or describe your responses.

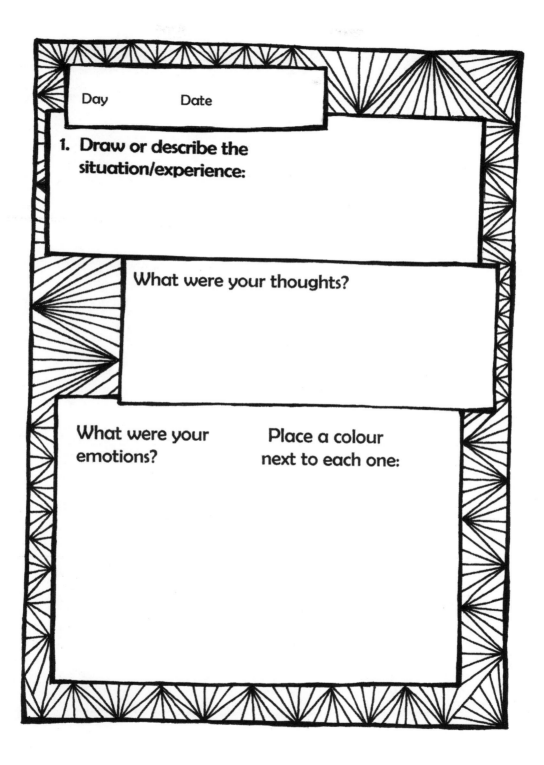

Day   Date

1. **Draw or describe the situation/experience:**

What were your thoughts?

What were your emotions?   **Place a colour next to each one:**

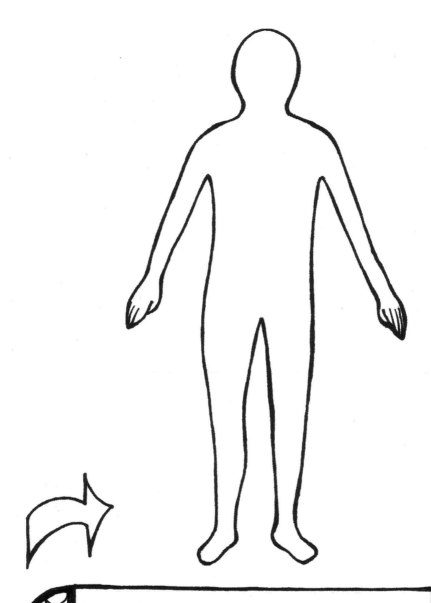

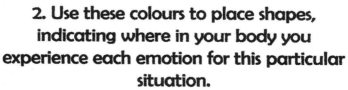

2. Use these colours to place shapes, indicating where in your body you experience each emotion for this particular situation.

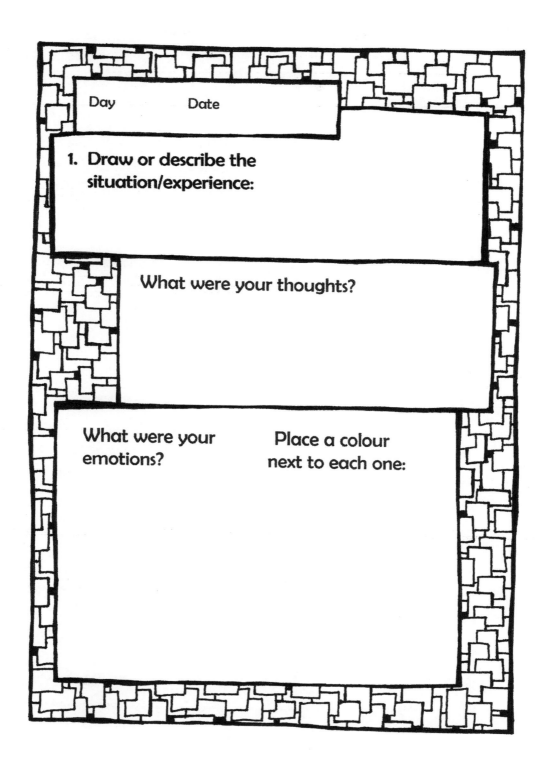

Day   Date

1. **Draw or describe the situation/experience:**

What were your thoughts?

What were your emotions?   **Place a colour next to each one:**

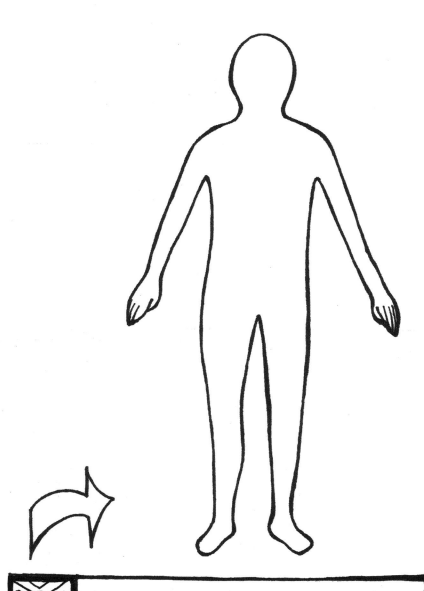

2. Use these colours to place shapes, indicating where in your body you experience each emotion for this particular situation.

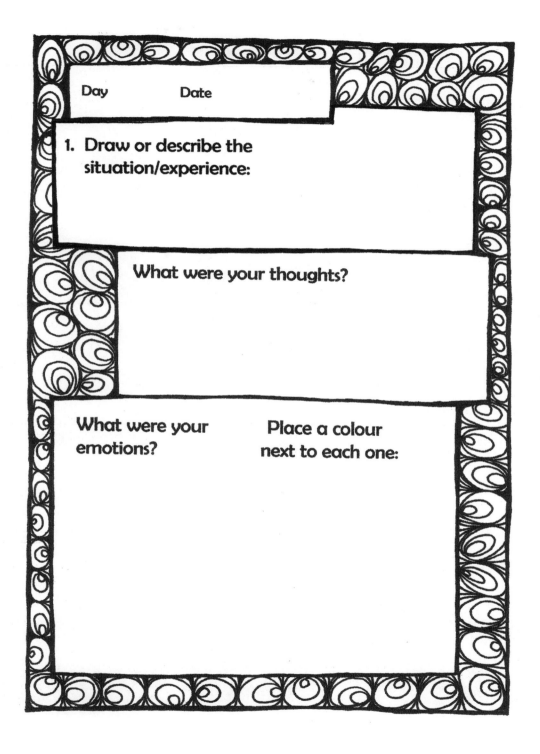

Day   Date

1. Draw or describe the situation/experience:

What were your thoughts?

What were your emotions?   Place a colour next to each one:

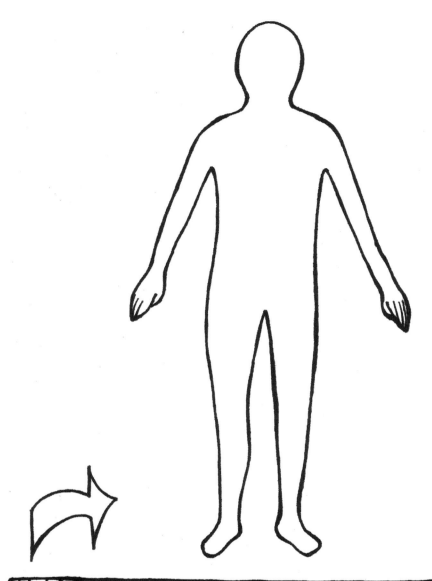

 2. Use these colours to place shapes, indicating where in your body you experience each emotion for this particular situation.

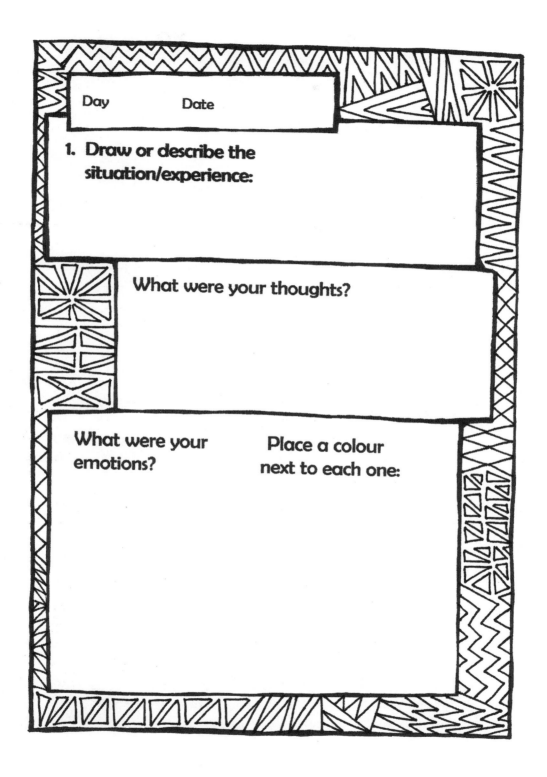

Day   Date

1. Draw or describe the
   situation/experience:

What were your thoughts?

What were your   Place a colour
emotions?   next to each one:

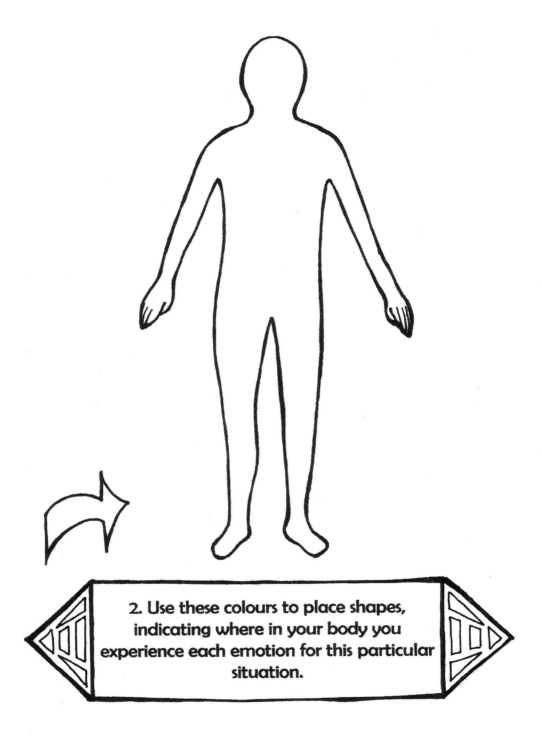

2. Use these colours to place shapes, indicating where in your body you experience each emotion for this particular situation.

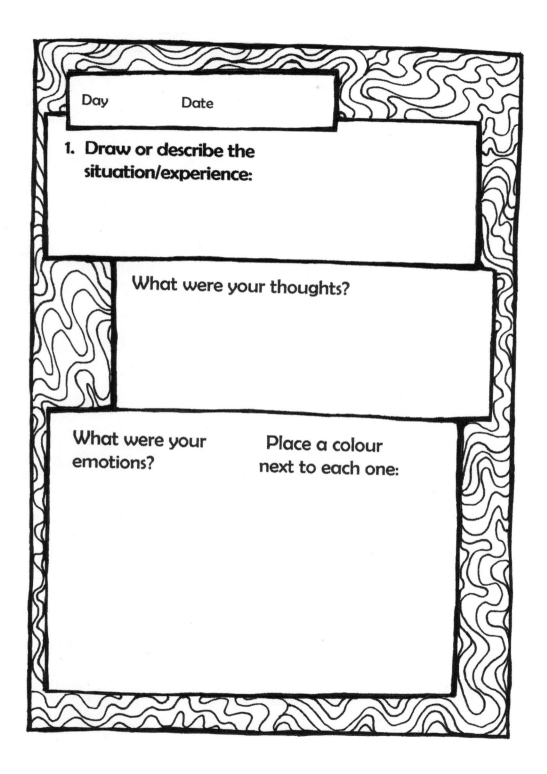

Day   Date

1. **Draw or describe the situation/experience:**

What were your thoughts?

What were your emotions?   **Place a colour next to each one:**

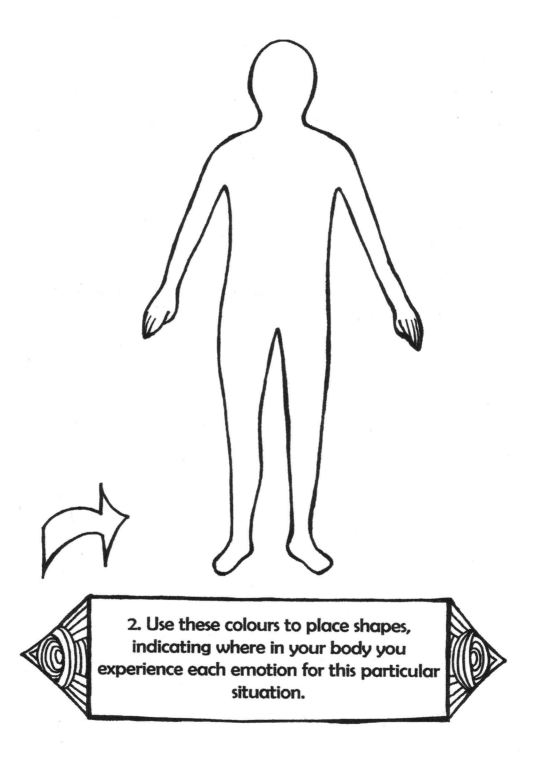

2. Use these colours to place shapes, indicating where in your body you experience each emotion for this particular situation.

4

Cognitions

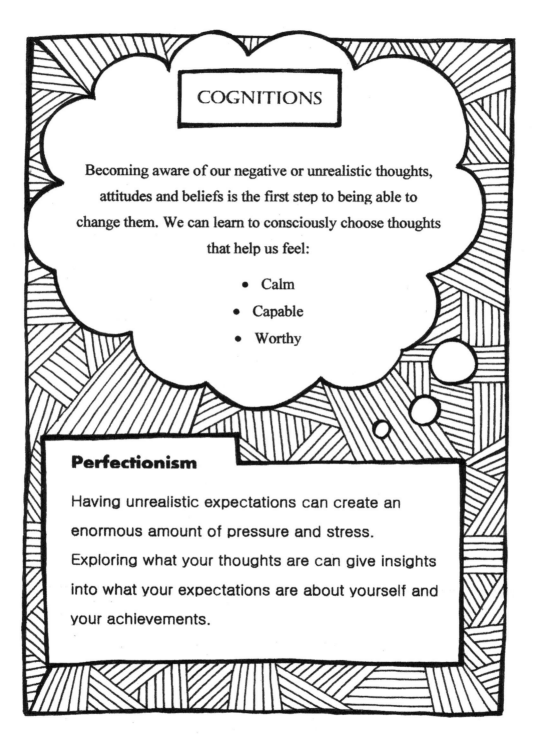

COGNITIONS

Becoming aware of our negative or unrealistic thoughts, attitudes and beliefs is the first step to being able to change them. We can learn to consciously choose thoughts that help us feel:

- Calm
- Capable
- Worthy

Perfectionism

Having unrealistic expectations can create an enormous amount of pressure and stress. Exploring what your thoughts are can give insights into what your expectations are about yourself and your achievements.

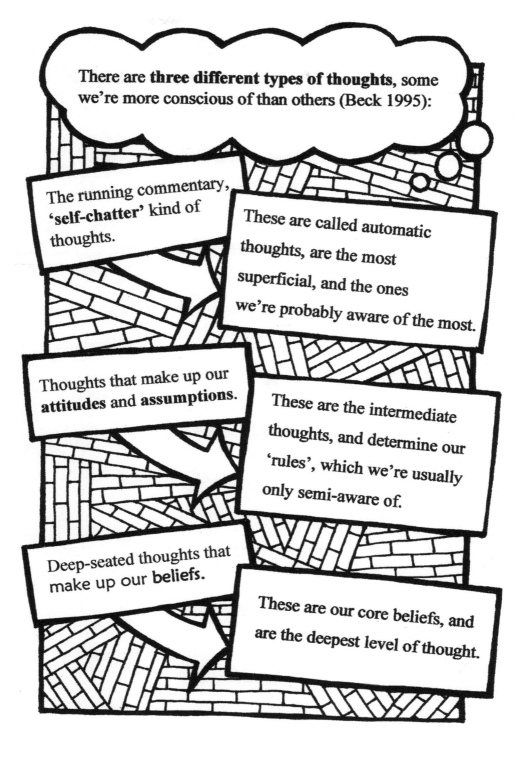

There are **three different types of thoughts**, some we're more conscious of than others (Beck 1995):

The running commentary, **'self-chatter'** kind of thoughts.

These are called automatic thoughts, are the most superficial, and the ones we're probably aware of the most.

Thoughts that make up our **attitudes** and **assumptions**.

These are the intermediate thoughts, and determine our 'rules', which we're usually only semi-aware of.

Deep-seated thoughts that make up our **beliefs.**

These are our core beliefs, and are the deepest level of thought.

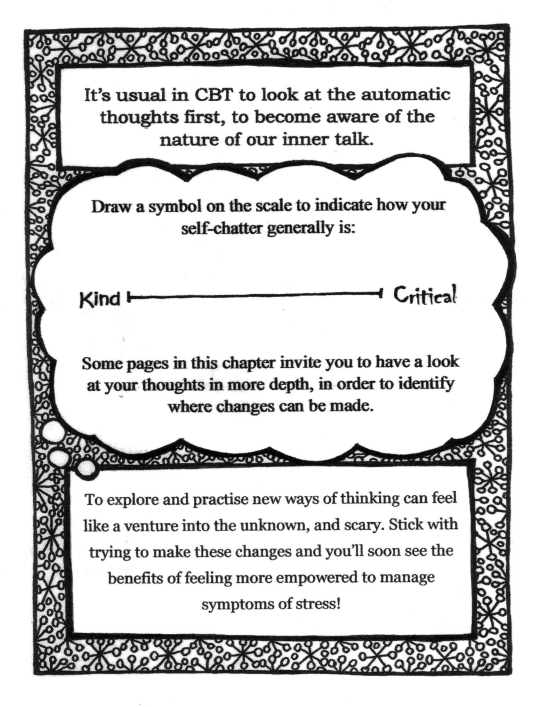

It's usual in CBT to look at the automatic thoughts first, to become aware of the nature of our inner talk.

Draw a symbol on the scale to indicate how your self-chatter generally is:

Kind ⊢————————————⊣ Critical

Some pages in this chapter invite you to have a look at your thoughts in more depth, in order to identify where changes can be made.

To explore and practise new ways of thinking can feel like a venture into the unknown, and scary. Stick with trying to make these changes and you'll soon see the benefits of feeling more empowered to manage symptoms of stress!

The *Compassion Triangle* was developed by Tagar (1995), who identified how we need to have **compassion, love and understanding** for ourselves. This can be expressed initially in our thoughts.

1. We feel low, down or upset

3. We seek out compassion, love and understanding for ourselves

2. We react; we criticise, judge, and blame ourselves for feeling this way and for our resulting behaviour

How we 'talk' to ourselves, *about* ourselves, is crucial to **how we feel**. If we're constantly being critical or judgemental about everything that we do, think, feel and say, then it will be difficult to feel calm and good about ourselves.

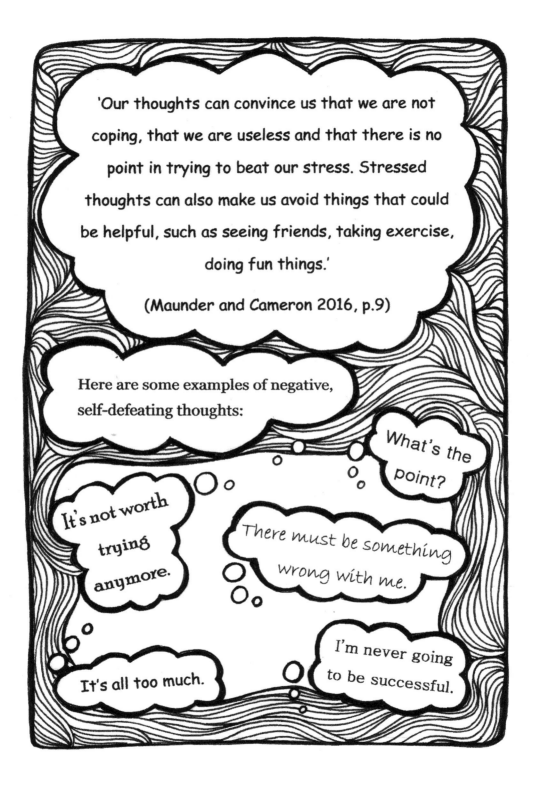

'Our thoughts can convince us that we are not coping, that we are useless and that there is no point in trying to beat our stress. Stressed thoughts can also make us avoid things that could be helpful, such as seeing friends, taking exercise, doing fun things.'

(Maunder and Cameron 2016, p.9)

Here are some examples of negative, self-defeating thoughts:

What's the point?

It's not worth trying anymore.

There must be something wrong with me.

I'm never going to be successful.

It's all too much.

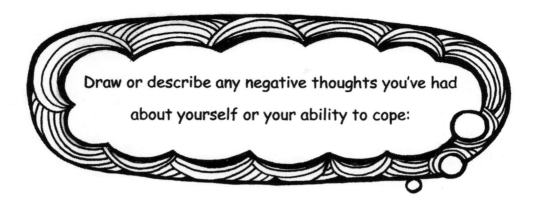

Draw or describe any negative thoughts you've had about yourself or your ability to cope:

Draw or describe some **nourishing and kind** thoughts you could adopt instead:

(If these are challenging for you to think of, imagine how you'd talk to yourself as a vulnerable child, or to a close friend who was upset.)

The following pages show some **self-soothing affirmations.**

As soon as you notice your inner self-talk becoming negative or critical, replace these with an affirmation, such as the ones on the next few pages.

Try repeating them over and over in your mind as you colour in or create an image for the phrase. The more often you practise, the easier it will be to remember them and you'll be able to more readily access them in future situations to help prevent symptoms from increasing.

Ideally these will start to develop into your beliefs.

The more familiar you become with positive thoughts and how they feel, the sooner you'll notice when your thoughts are not soothing or nurturing.

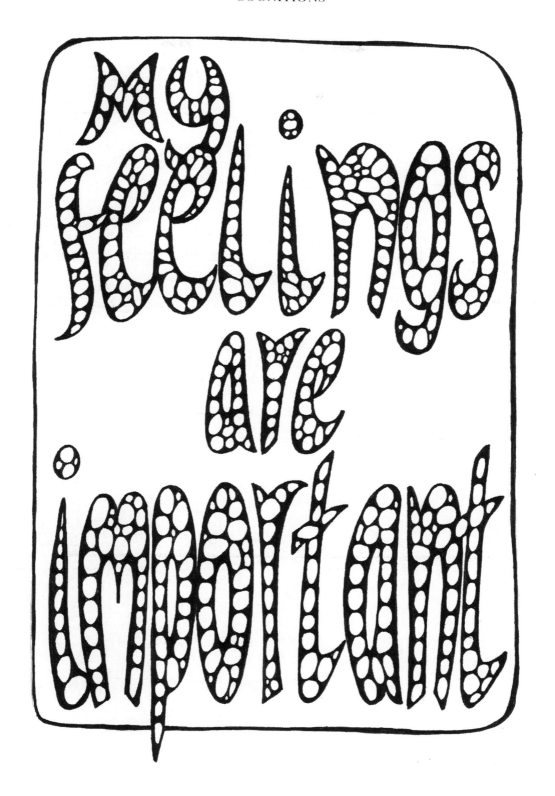

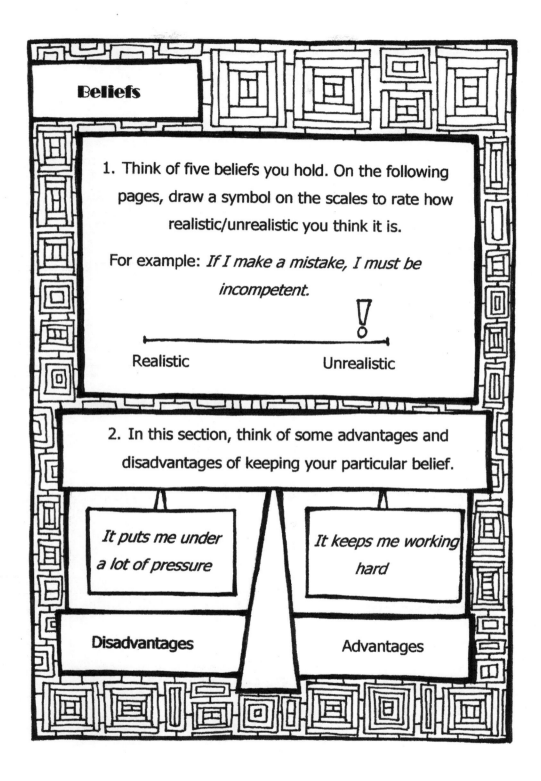

Beliefs

1. Think of five beliefs you hold. On the following pages, draw a symbol on the scales to rate how realistic/unrealistic you think it is.

For example: *If I make a mistake, I must be incompetent.*

Realistic   Unrealistic

2. In this section, think of some advantages and disadvantages of keeping your particular belief.

It puts me under a lot of pressure

It keeps me working hard

Disadvantages   Advantages

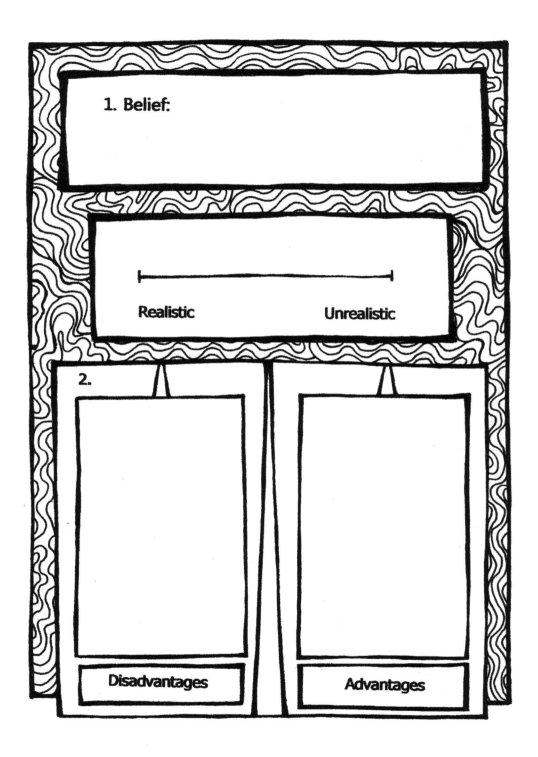

1. Belief:

Realistic   Unrealistic

2.

Disadvantages   Advantages

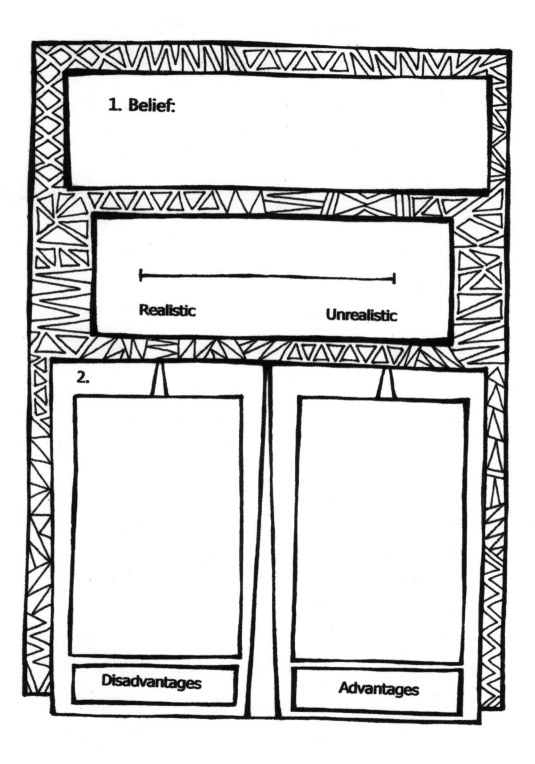

1. Belief:

Realistic   Unrealistic

2.

Disadvantages

Advantages

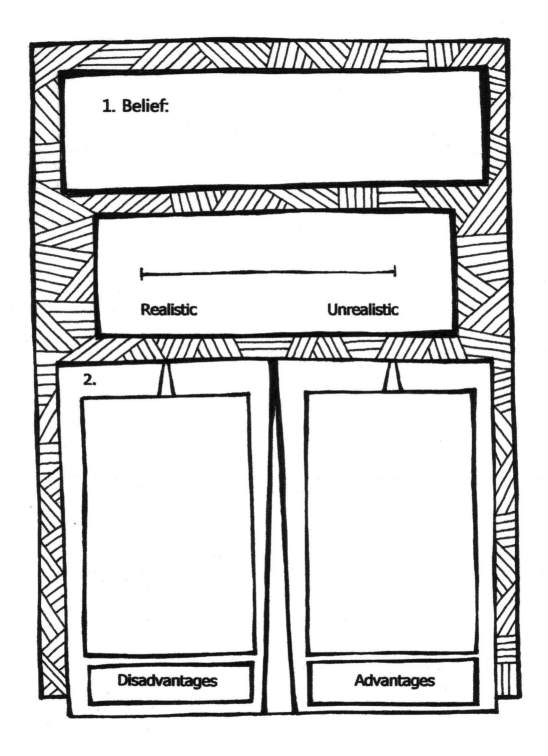

1. Belief:

Realistic   Unrealistic

2.

Disadvantages   Advantages

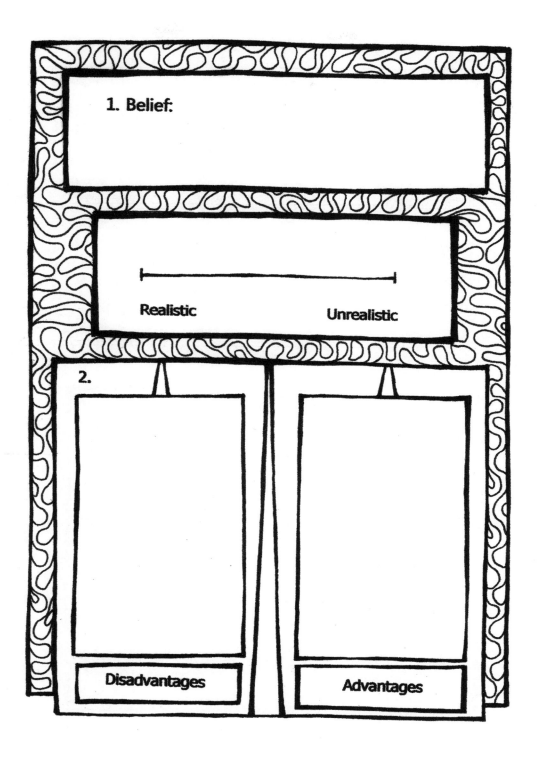

1. Belief:

Realistic   Unrealistic

2.

Disadvantages   Advantages

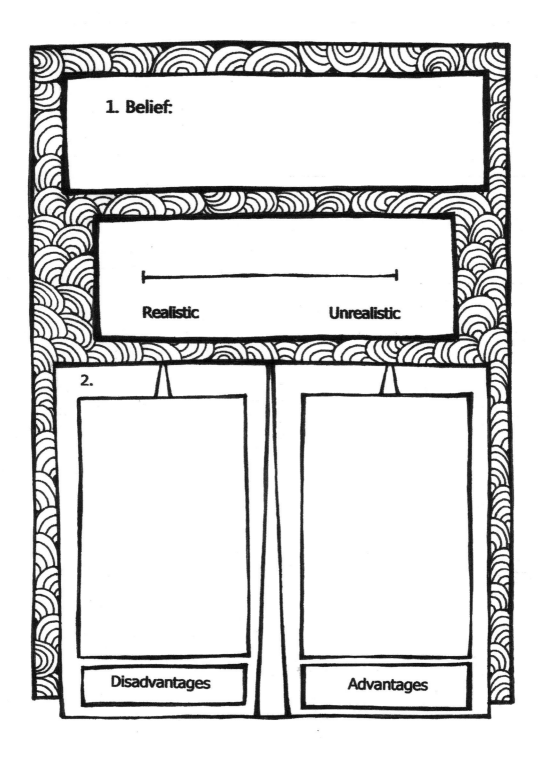

1. Belief:

Realistic   Unrealistic

2.

Disadvantages   Advantages

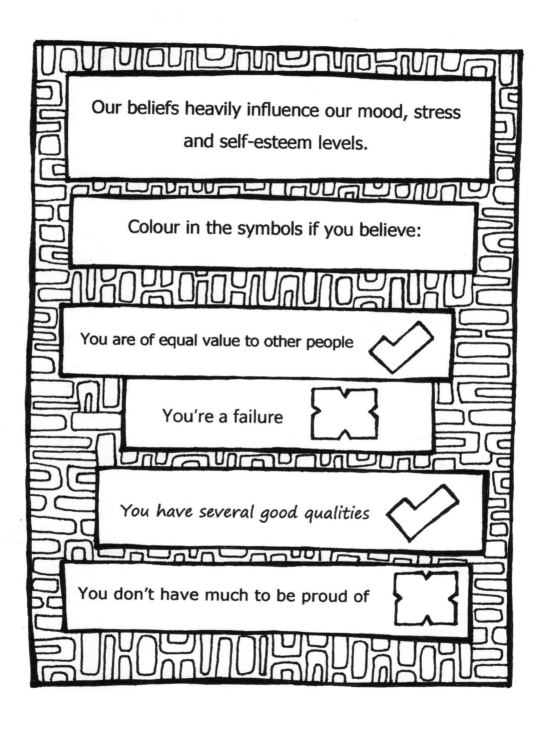

Our beliefs heavily influence our mood, stress and self-esteem levels.

Colour in the symbols if you believe:

You are of equal value to other people

You're a failure

You have several good qualities

You don't have much to be proud of

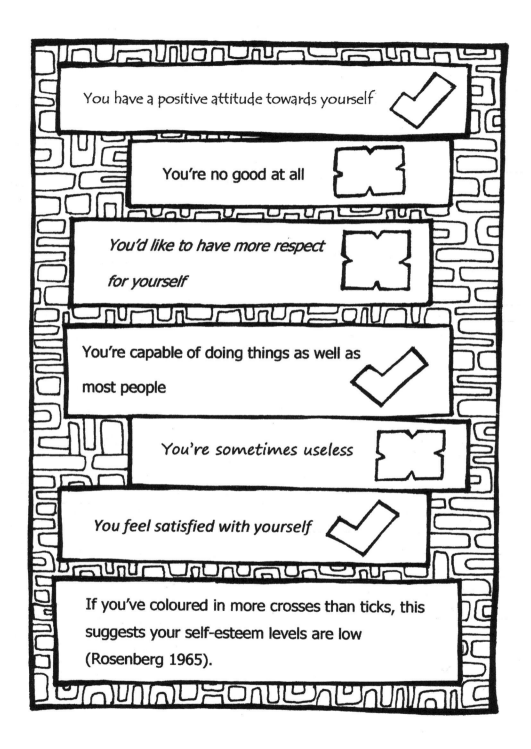

You have a positive attitude towards yourself

You're no good at all

You'd like to have more respect for yourself

You're capable of doing things as well as most people

You're sometimes useless

You feel satisfied with yourself

If you've coloured in more crosses than ticks, this suggests your self-esteem levels are low (Rosenberg 1965).

5

Emotions

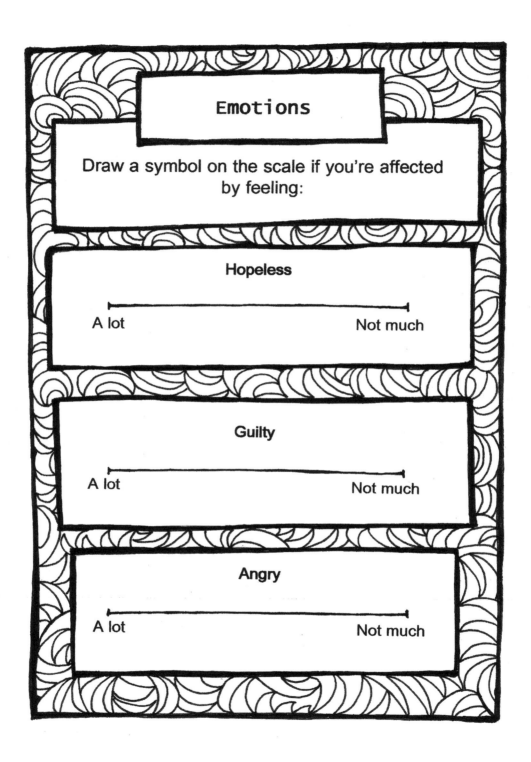

Emotions

Draw a symbol on the scale if you're affected by feeling:

Hopeless

A lot   Not much

Guilty

A lot   Not much

Angry

A lot   Not much

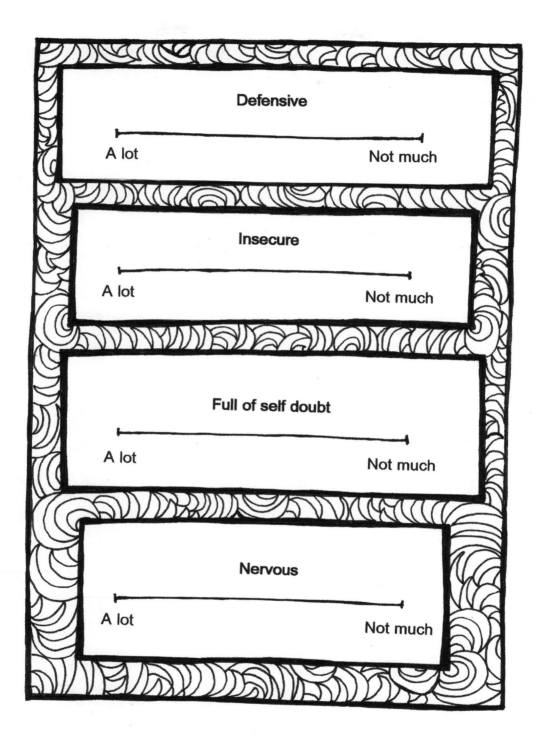

Defensive

A lot   Not much

Insecure

A lot   Not much

Full of self doubt

A lot   Not much

Nervous

A lot   Not much

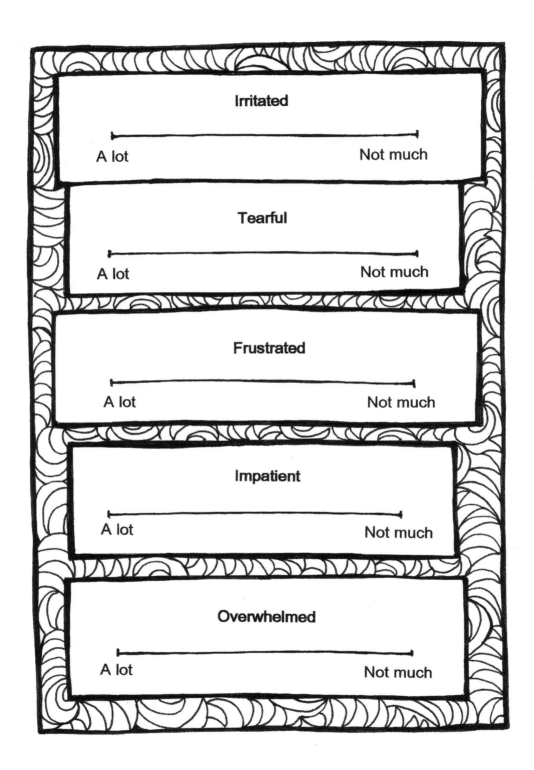

Beliefs about emotions

You can only start to **take control** of your emotions if you **believe that you can**, and this is essential for lowering emotional distress.

(Winch 2018)

Draw a symbol on the scale to show whether you believe your emotions are fixed or malleable:

|————————————————————|

Fixed   Malleable

'Beliefs that individuals hold about whether emotions are malleable or fixed may play a crucial role in individuals' emotional experiences and their engagement in changing their emotions.'

(Kneeland *et al.* 2016, pp.81–88)

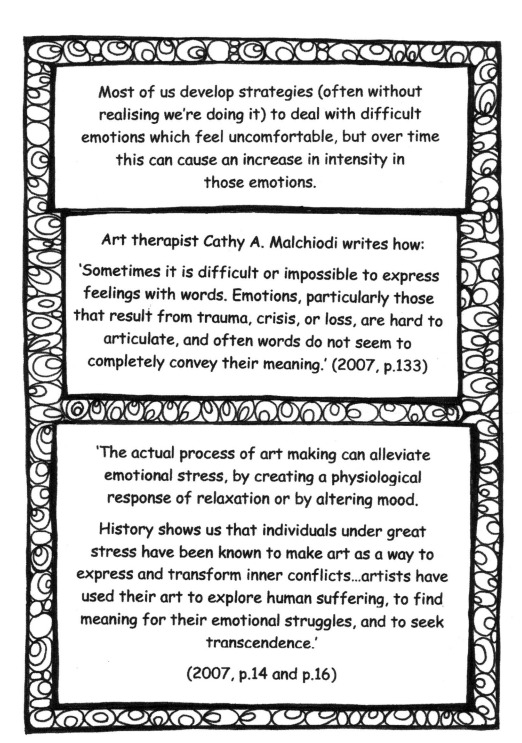

Most of us develop strategies (often without realising we're doing it) to deal with difficult emotions which feel uncomfortable, but over time this can cause an increase in intensity in those emotions.

Art therapist Cathy A. Malchiodi writes how:

'Sometimes it is difficult or impossible to express feelings with words. Emotions, particularly those that result from trauma, crisis, or loss, are hard to articulate, and often words do not seem to completely convey their meaning.' (2007, p.133)

'The actual process of art making can alleviate emotional stress, by creating a physiological response of relaxation or by altering mood.

History shows us that individuals under great stress have been known to make art as a way to express and transform inner conflicts...artists have used their art to explore human suffering, to find meaning for their emotional struggles, and to seek transcendence.'

(2007, p.14 and p.16)

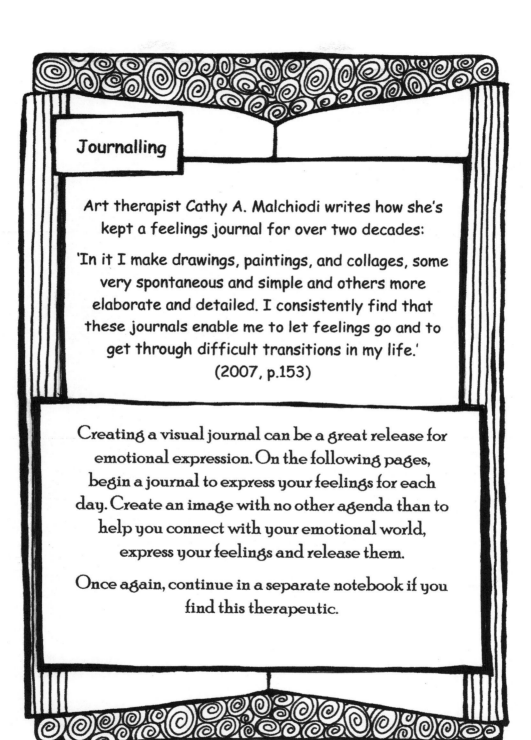

Journalling

Art therapist Cathy A. Malchiodi writes how she's kept a feelings journal for over two decades:

'In it I make drawings, paintings, and collages, some very spontaneous and simple and others more elaborate and detailed. I consistently find that these journals enable me to let feelings go and to get through difficult transitions in my life.'
(2007, p.153)

Creating a visual journal can be a great release for emotional expression. On the following pages, begin a journal to express your feelings for each day. Create an image with no other agenda than to help you connect with your emotional world, express your feelings and release them.

Once again, continue in a separate notebook if you find this therapeutic.

Monday: *I feel...*

Tuesday: *I feel...*

Wednesday: I feel...

Thursday: *I feel...*

Saturday: I feel...

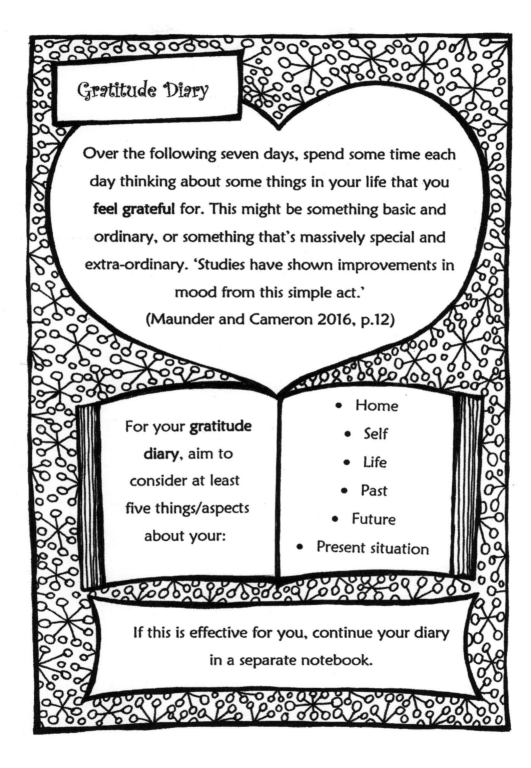

Gratitude Diary

Over the following seven days, spend some time each day thinking about some things in your life that you **feel grateful** for. This might be something basic and ordinary, or something that's massively special and extra-ordinary. 'Studies have shown improvements in mood from this simple act.'
(Maunder and Cameron 2016, p.12)

For your **gratitude diary**, aim to consider at least five things/aspects about your:

- Home
- Self
- Life
- Past
- Future
- Present situation

If this is effective for you, continue your diary in a separate notebook.

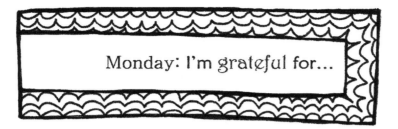

Tuesday: I'm grateful for...

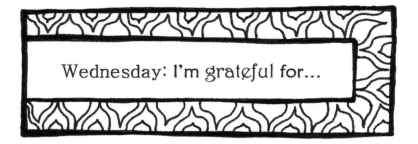

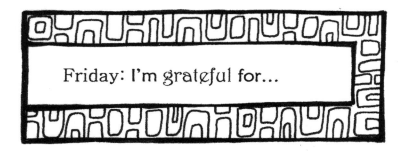

Saturday: I'm grateful for...

6

Behaviours

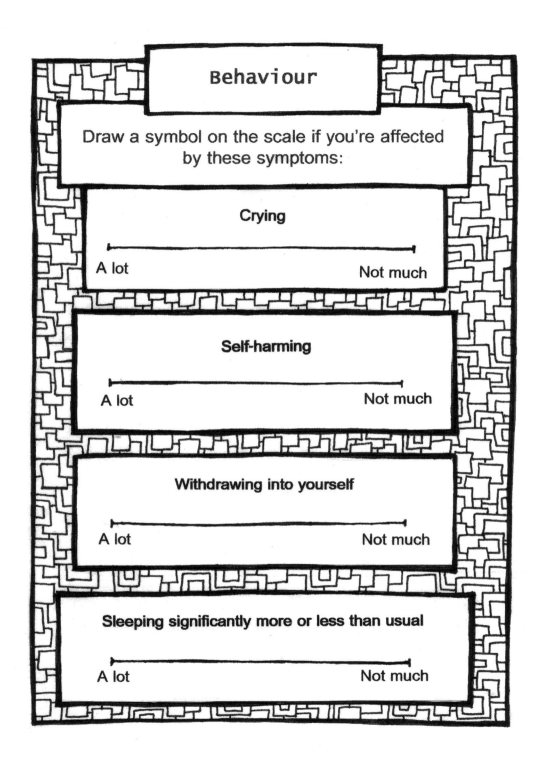

Behaviour

Draw a symbol on the scale if you're affected by these symptoms:

Crying

A lot ———————————————— Not much

Self-harming

A lot ———————————————— Not much

Withdrawing into yourself

A lot ———————————————— Not much

Sleeping significantly more or less than usual

A lot ———————————————— Not much

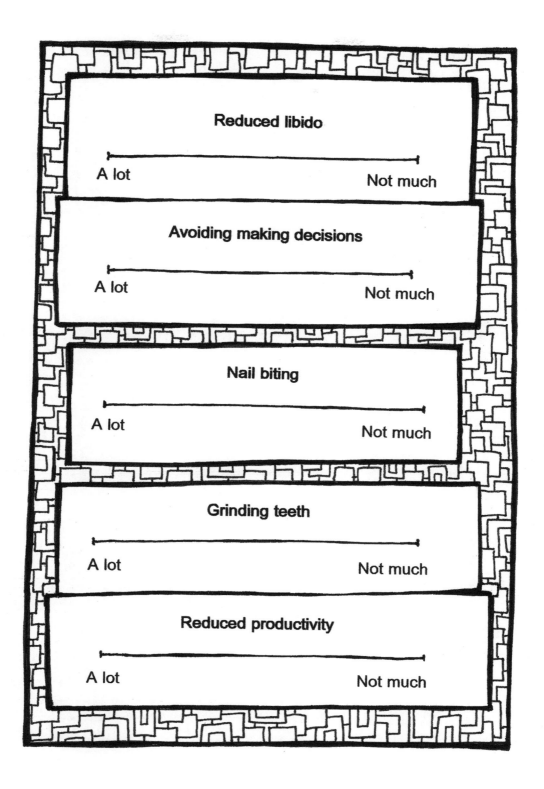

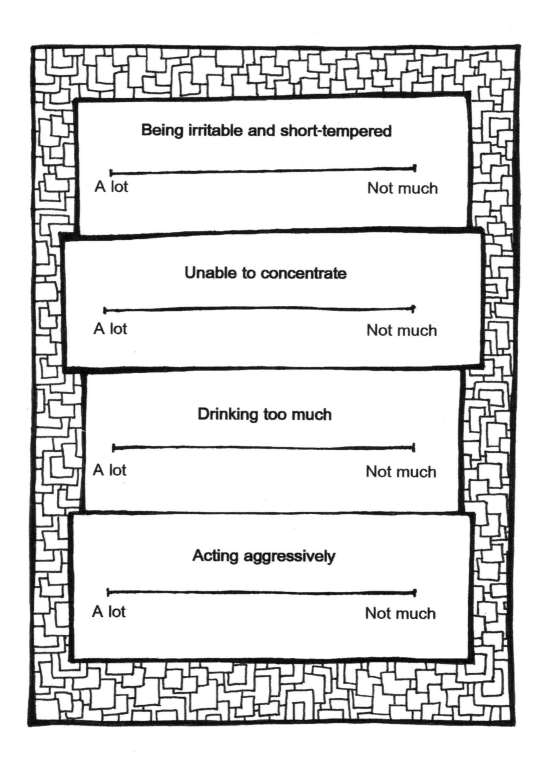

Some of the most common techniques to *reduce* symptoms of stress from a behavioural perspective are by:

- Exploring how to limit or reduce **pressures**
- Increasing effectiveness of **time management**
- Increasing time spent **relaxing**
- Increasing time spent **exercising**

Prioritising

Consider your week ahead. Use the following page to draw or describe the tasks necessary for next week, and separate them into priorities, leaving out regular daily tasks. This can help to explore if any external pressures can be reduced.

Tasks for the week ahead:

Urgent/ essential	Important	Can be done another time

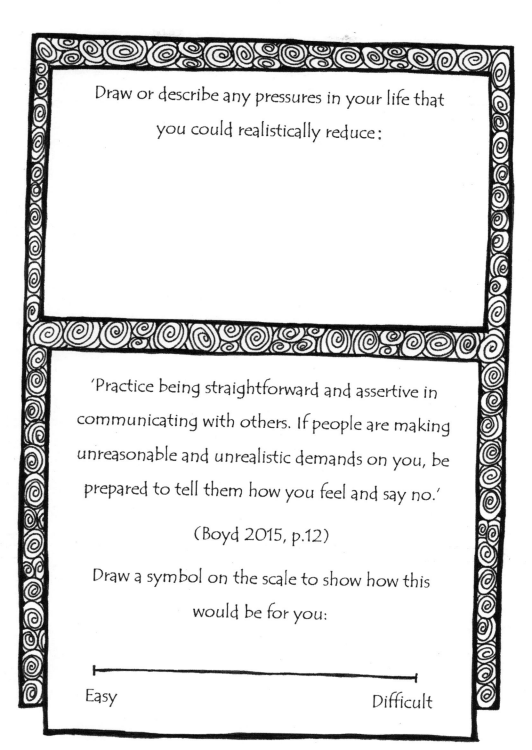

Draw or describe any pressures in your life that you could realistically reduce:

'Practice being straightforward and assertive in communicating with others. If people are making unreasonable and unrealistic demands on you, be prepared to tell them how you feel and say no.'

(Boyd 2015, p.12)

Draw a symbol on the scale to show how this would be for you:

Easy   Difficult

Create an image – realistic or abstract – of how you feel after you've been successfully assertive:

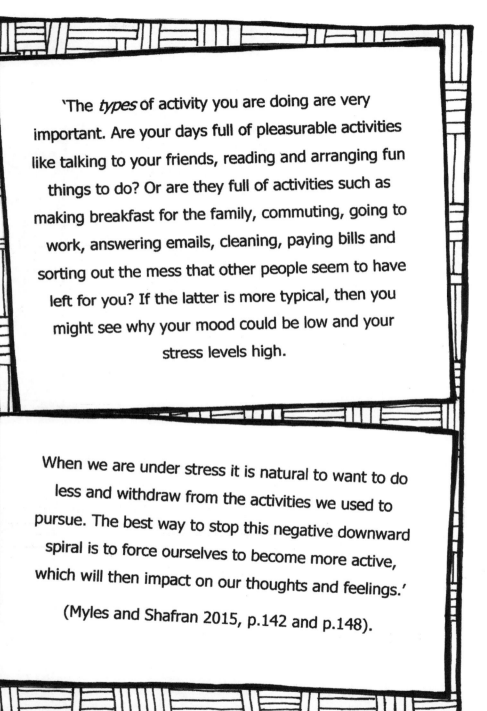

'The *types* of activity you are doing are very important. Are your days full of pleasurable activities like talking to your friends, reading and arranging fun things to do? Or are they full of activities such as making breakfast for the family, commuting, going to work, answering emails, cleaning, paying bills and sorting out the mess that other people seem to have left for you? If the latter is more typical, then you might see why your mood could be low and your stress levels high.

When we are under stress it is natural to want to do less and withdraw from the activities we used to pursue. The best way to stop this negative downward spiral is to force ourselves to become more active, which will then impact on our thoughts and feelings.'

(Myles and Shafran 2015, p.142 and p.148).

MAKE A PLAN

On the following pages, complete the daily plans to encourage effective time management. Include necessary daily tasks and commitments, and use the information from the priority page to decide what is absolutely necessary to include in your week. Doing this can help to feel more in control of your time. If this is helpful for you, complete further weeks' planning.

It can be tempting to decrease time spent sleeping, relaxing and exercising if we have intense time pressure. Paradoxically, if we make time for these, our productivity can be enhanced because we'll be more rested and relaxed.

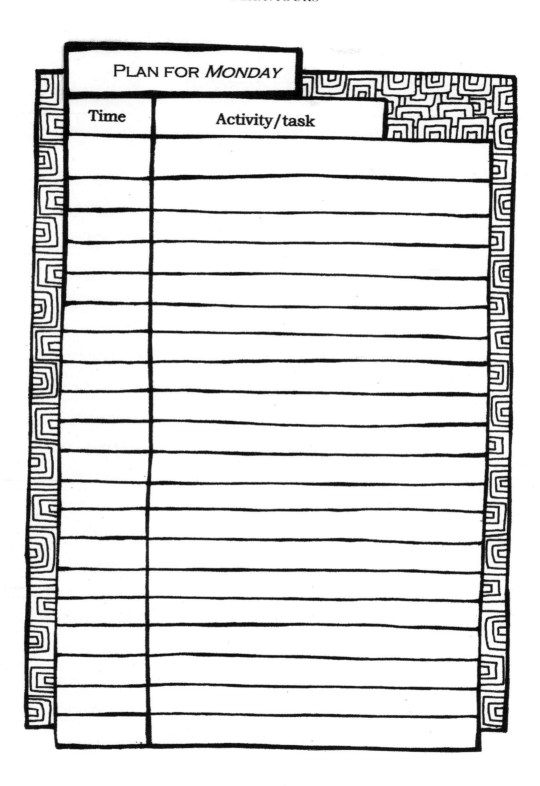

PLAN FOR *MONDAY*

Time	Activity/task

PLAN FOR *TUESDAY*

Time	Activity/task

PLAN FOR *WEDNESDAY*

Time	Activity/task

PLAN FOR *THURSDAY*

Time	Activity/task

PLAN FOR *FRIDAY*

Time	Activity/task

PLAN FOR *SATURDAY*

Time	Activity/task

Time	Activity/task

PLAN FOR *SUNDAY*

1. You have an entire day free of commitments and responsibilities. Create an image of how you'd spend your time:

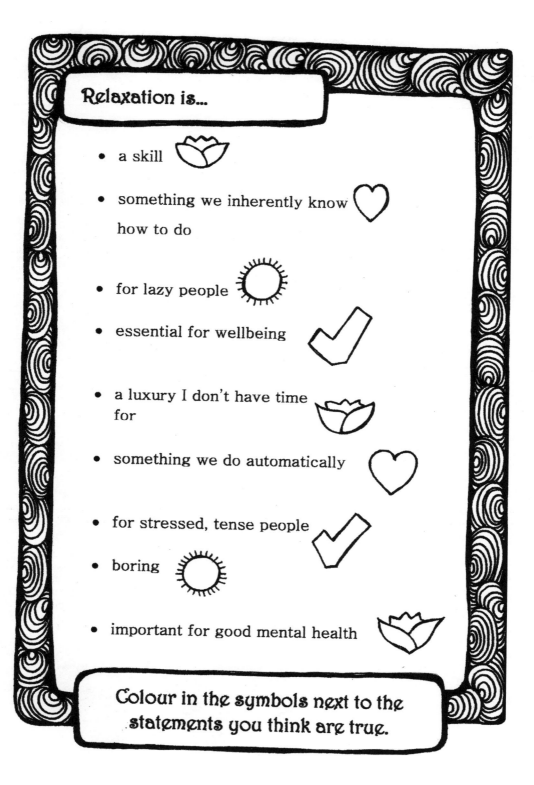

Relaxation is...

- a skill

- something we inherently know how to do

- for lazy people

- essential for wellbeing

- a luxury I don't have time for

- something we do automatically

- for stressed, tense people

- boring

- important for good mental health

Colour in the symbols next to the statements you think are true.

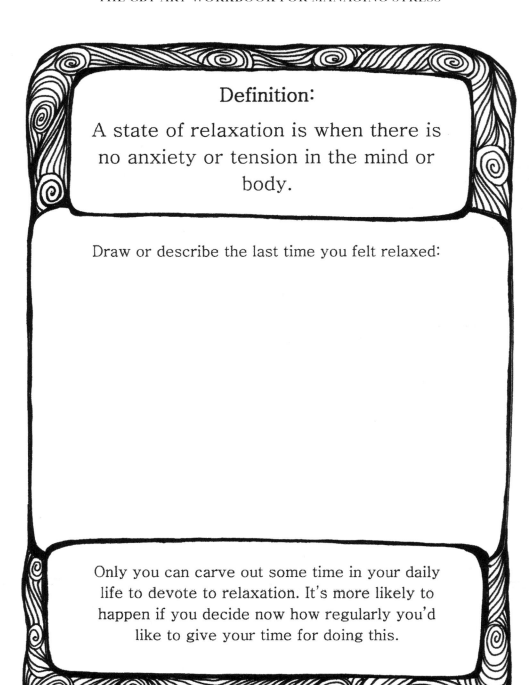

Definition:

A state of relaxation is when there is no anxiety or tension in the mind or body.

Draw or describe the last time you felt relaxed:

Only you can carve out some time in your daily life to devote to relaxation. It's more likely to happen if you decide now how regularly you'd like to give your time for doing this.

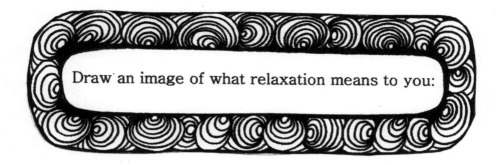

Draw an image of what relaxation means to you:

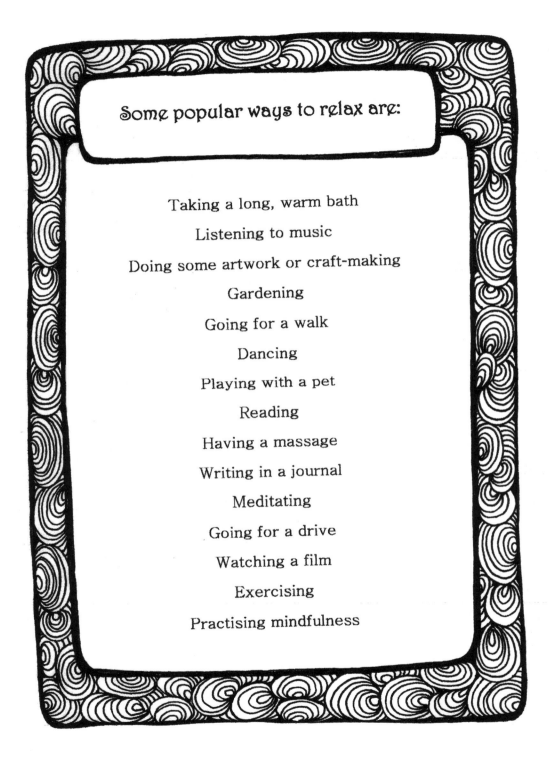

Some popular ways to relax are:

Taking a long, warm bath

Listening to music

Doing some artwork or craft-making

Gardening

Going for a walk

Dancing

Playing with a pet

Reading

Having a massage

Writing in a journal

Meditating

Going for a drive

Watching a film

Exercising

Practising mindfulness

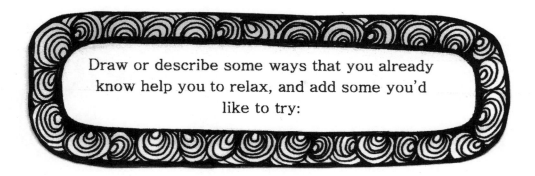

Draw or describe some ways that you already know help you to relax, and add some you'd like to try:

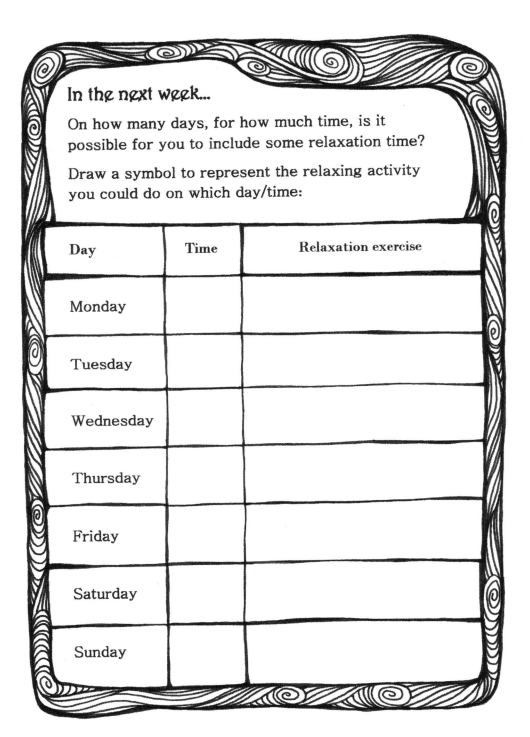

In the next week...

On how many days, for how much time, is it possible for you to include some relaxation time?

Draw a symbol to represent the relaxing activity you could do on which day/time:

Day	Time	Relaxation exercise
Monday		
Tuesday		
Wednesday		
Thursday		
Friday		
Saturday		
Sunday		

Achievements

A common feature when we're overwhelmed with pressure is to focus on what we're *not* doing, or *haven't* yet achieved, instead of what we **are** managing to do. It's helpful to remember how experiencing stress can reduce our productivity levels. If tasks are more challenging now because we're also dealing with stress, then it's a greater achievement to accomplish those tasks.

Completing **any task** that is challenging, however small, **is an achievement!**

7

Physiology

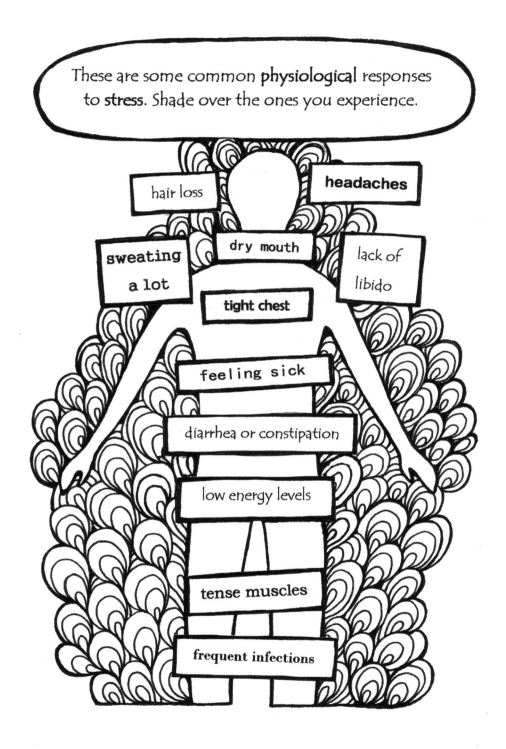

These are some common **physiological** responses to **stress**. Shade over the ones you experience.

hair loss

headaches

sweating a lot

dry mouth

lack of libido

tight chest

feeling sick

diarrhea or constipation

low energy levels

tense muscles

frequent infections

Physiology

Clinical psychologists Lesley Maunder and Lorna Cameron (2016, p.3) write:

'Physical symptoms are mostly linked to our ancient survival strategy, the fight or flight response. This releases hormones such as **cortisol** and **adrenaline** into our body, literally preparing us to fight or flee. The pressures we face nowadays are not usually helped by this response. We can't usually flee from debt, deadlines or stressful life events!

Many people are quite worried when they feel these symptoms, and think they may be signs of a serious physical or mental health problem, such as having a heart attack or cracking up. They are not dangerous and are in fact very common.'

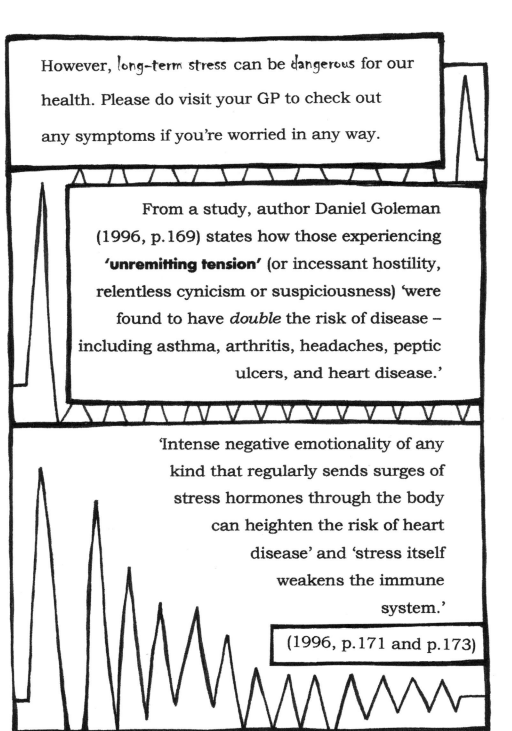

However, long-term stress can be dangerous for our health. Please do visit your GP to check out any symptoms if you're worried in any way.

From a study, author Daniel Goleman (1996, p.169) states how those experiencing **'unremitting tension'** (or incessant hostility, relentless cynicism or suspiciousness) 'were found to have *double* the risk of disease – including asthma, arthritis, headaches, peptic ulcers, and heart disease.'

'Intense negative emotionality of any kind that regularly sends surges of stress hormones through the body can heighten the risk of heart disease' and 'stress itself weakens the immune system.'

(1996, p.171 and p.173)

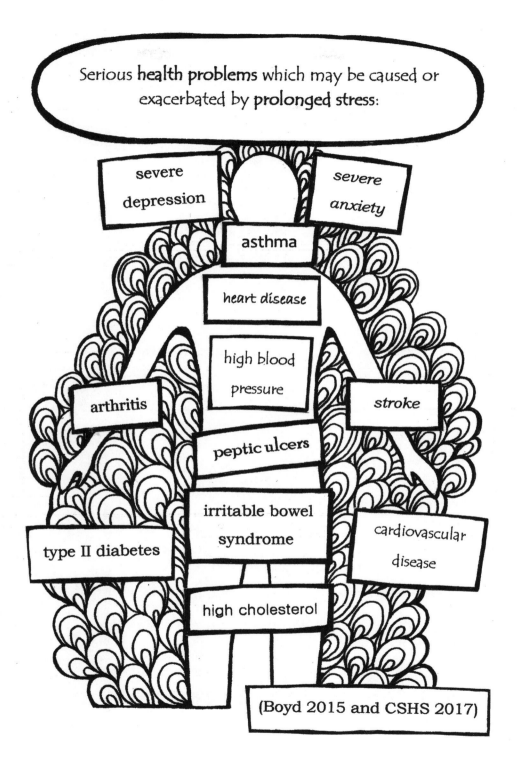

Serious **health problems** which may be caused or exacerbated by **prolonged stress:**

severe depression

severe anxiety

asthma

heart disease

high blood pressure

arthritis

stroke

peptic ulcers

irritable bowel syndrome

type II diabetes

cardiovascular disease

high cholesterol

(Boyd 2015 and CSHS 2017)

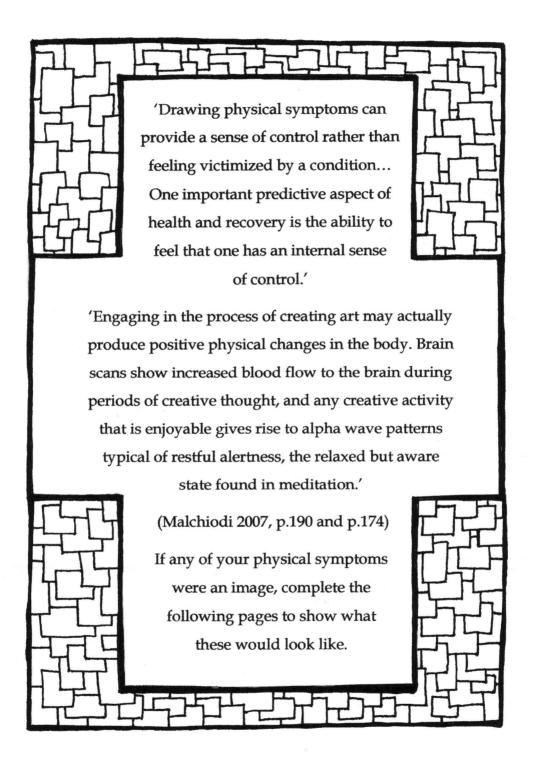

'Drawing physical symptoms can provide a sense of control rather than feeling victimized by a condition… One important predictive aspect of health and recovery is the ability to feel that one has an internal sense of control.'

'Engaging in the process of creating art may actually produce positive physical changes in the body. Brain scans show increased blood flow to the brain during periods of creative thought, and any creative activity that is enjoyable gives rise to alpha wave patterns typical of restful alertness, the relaxed but aware state found in meditation.'

(Malchiodi 2007, p.190 and p.174)

If any of your physical symptoms were an image, complete the following pages to show what these would look like.

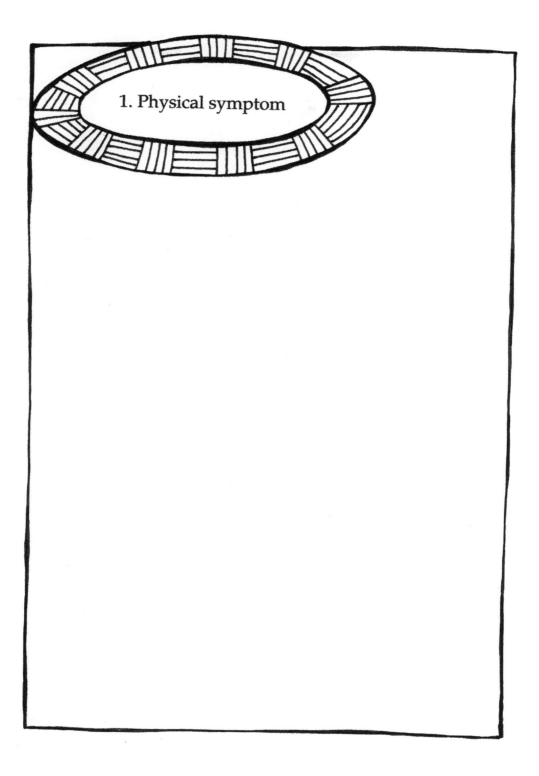

1. Physical symptom

2. Physical symptom

3. Physical symptom

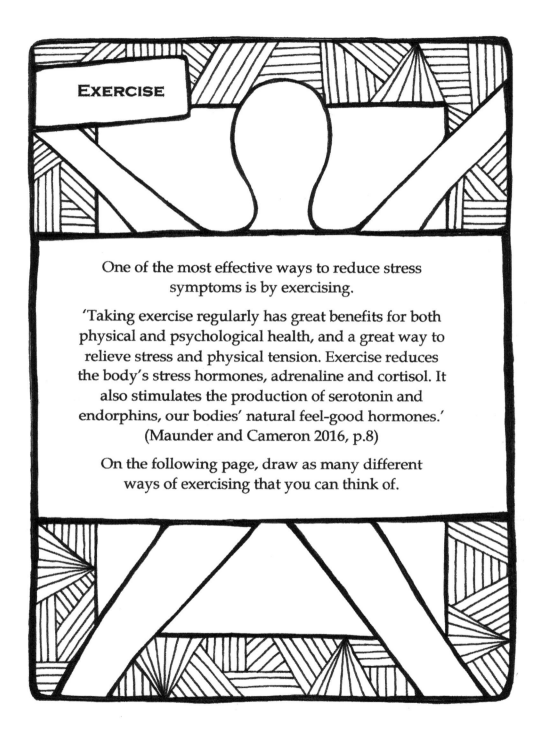

EXERCISE

One of the most effective ways to reduce stress symptoms is by exercising.

'Taking exercise regularly has great benefits for both physical and psychological health, and a great way to relieve stress and physical tension. Exercise reduces the body's stress hormones, adrenaline and cortisol. It also stimulates the production of serotonin and endorphins, our bodies' natural feel-good hormones.' (Maunder and Cameron 2016, p.8)

On the following page, draw as many different ways of exercising that you can think of.

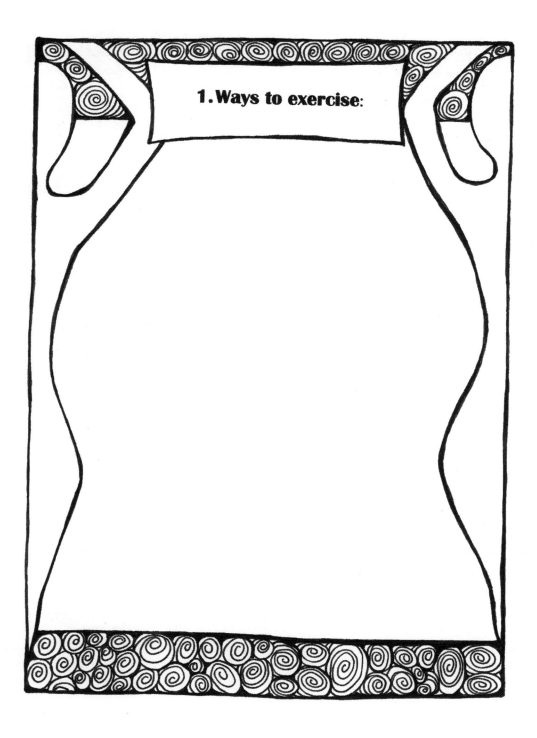

1. Ways to exercise:

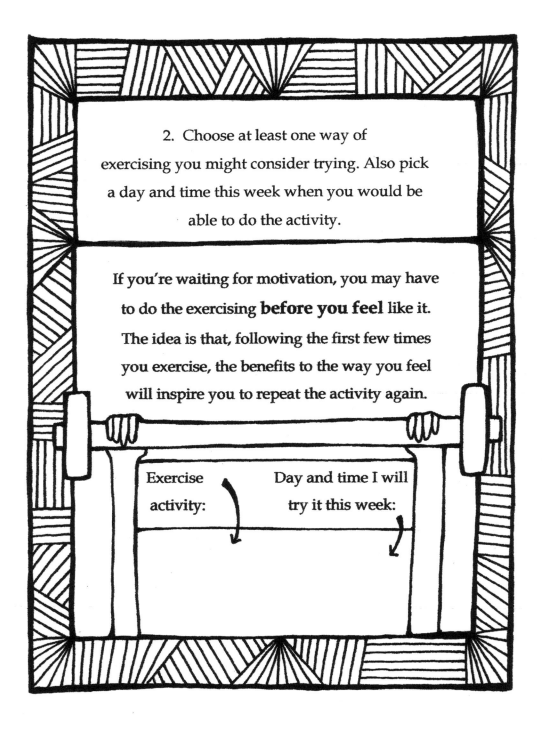

2. Choose at least one way of exercising you might consider trying. Also pick a day and time this week when you would be able to do the activity.

If you're waiting for motivation, you may have to do the exercising **before you feel** like it. The idea is that, following the first few times you exercise, the benefits to the way you feel will inspire you to repeat the activity again.

Exercise activity:

Day and time I will try it this week:

Close your eyes and think of a place where you feel safe and content. Spending time in this imaginary place will relax your body. What can you see, hear, smell and touch? What's the weather like? Are you with others or alone?

What does your safe place look like?

8

Less Stress

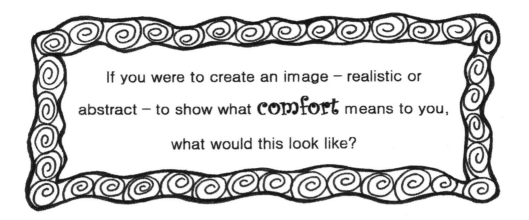

If you were to create an image – realistic or abstract – to show what **comfort** means to you, what would this look like?

If you were to create an image – realistic or abstract – to show what **relief** means to you, what would this look like?

If you were to create an image – realistic or abstract –

to show what **serenity** means to you, what

would this look like?

If you were to create an image – realistic or abstract – to show what *peace* means to you, what would this look like?

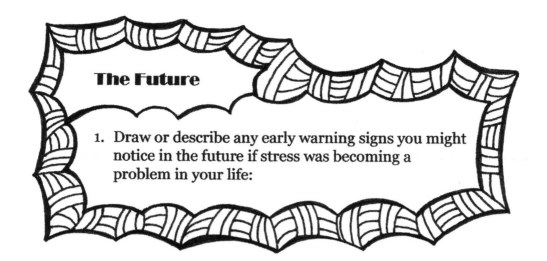

The Future

1. Draw or describe any early warning signs you might notice in the future if stress was becoming a problem in your life:

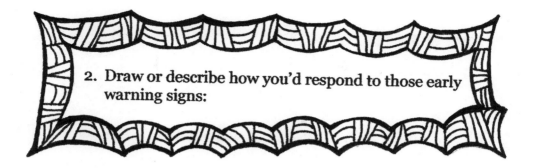

2. Draw or describe how you'd respond to those early warning signs:

Congratulations!

By making efforts such as completing this workbook and putting in time to focus on changing and lowering your levels of stress, you are demonstrating how much you're willing to take more control of...

- your life
- your wellbeing
- your mental health
- your future
- the person you want to be

...and in turn, this takes courage and strength. I hope you can acknowledge this for the achievement that it already is!

References

Barford, D. (2018) 'Dark night of the soul.' *Therapy Today*, 29(6): 35.

Beck, J.S. (1995) *Cognitive Therapy: Basics and Beyond.* New York, NY: Guilford Press.

Boyd, R. (2015) *How to Manage Stress.* Available at: www.mind.org.uk/media/1993364/how-to-manage-stress_2015.pdf.

Centre for Studies on Human Stress (CSHS) (2017) 'Stress'. Available at: https://humanstress.ca/stress.

Cohen, S., Kamarck, T. and Mermelstein, M. (1983) 'A global measure of perceived stress.' *Journal of Health and Social Behaviour*, 24(4): 386–396.

Goleman, D. (1996) *Emotional Intelligence.* London: Bloomsbury.

Kneeland, E.T., Dovidio, J.F., Joormann, J. and Clark, M.S. (2016) 'Emotion malleability beliefs, emotion regulation, and psychopathology: Integrating affective and clinical science.' *Clinical Psychology Review*, April, 45:81–88. Available at: www.ncbi.nlm.nih.gov/pubmed/27086086.

Labour Force Survey (2013) *Stress and Psychological Disorders in Great Britain 2013.* Health and Safety Executive. Available at: https://static.guim.co.uk/ni/1412687972727/stress-1.pdf.

London, P. (1989) *No More Secondhand Art: Awakening the Artist Within.* Boston, MA: Shambala.

Malchiodi, C.A. (2007) *The Art Therapy Sourcebook.* New York, NY: McGraw Hill.

Maunder, L. and Cameron, L. (2016) *Stress.* Newcastle: Northumberland, Tyne and Wear NHS Foundation Trust.

Myles, P. and Shafran, R. (2015) *The CBT Handbook.* London: Robinson.

Neenan, M. and Dryden, W. (2004) *Cognitive Therapy: 100 Key Points and Techniques.* Hove: Brunner Routledge.

Rosenberg, M. (1965) *Society and the Adolescent Self Image.* Princeton, NJ: Princeton University Press.

Tagar, Y. (1995) 'Compassion: A path of self-healing.' *Golden Age Magazine*, Jul/Aug, 25–28.

Winch, G. (2018) 'Why You Should Believe You Can Control Your Emotions' *Psychology Today* (posted 5 Sep 18). Available at: www.psychologytoday.com/gb/blog/the-squeaky-wheel/201809/why-you-should-believe-you-can-control-your-emotions.

YouGov (2019) Mental Health Foundation Study. Available at: www.mentalhealth.org.uk/statistics/mental-health-statistics-stress.